Words of Praise for
A VERY HUNGRY GI

*"Jessica Weiner's book, **A Very Hungry Girl,** speaks to the hunger that almost every woman carries. All of us can relate to these stories that few will speak about. I applaud her work in helping women cross the barrier from self-hatred to self-love. This is a must-read for anyone working with the young."*

— **Louise L. Hay,** the bestselling author of *You Can Heal Your Life*

"Jessica Weiner sheds light on issues that teens and parents shroud in private darkness. With compassion, empathy, and humor, she enables you to examine, address, and ultimately heal."

— **John Edward,** host of *Crossing Over with John Edward;* author of *One Last Time* and *Crossing Over*

"Jessica Weiner has reached a very self-actualized state of being at a very young age. I'm so pleased that she's using her strength and intelligence to enlighten others in this wonderful book. Jessica has prioritized and come out a winner, teacher, and friend to all who read her words."

— **Janeane Garofalo,** TV and film actress

"We <u>need</u> Jessica and her voice! As the mother of a teenage girl and a member of the media, I know the pressure of growing up with the constant scrutiny of a judgmental society. Jessica's message is nourishing and validating. We need to clone her and have her on constant standby! Thank you, Jessica, for your courage and wisdom."

— **Leeza Gibbons,** TV journalist and host

*"In **A Very Hungry Girl,** author Jessica Weiner gives readers an unstintingly honest account of her struggles with bulimia. Ms. Weiner is forthright about her own culpability in succumbing to societal pressures to be thin, but she also helps us see just how powerful these messages are. Her account of other young women whose lives she touched with her drama-outreach work, and her practical suggestions of 'Take-Away Tools,' make this book one I will promote to the many moms and daughters I encounter with various eating disorders."*

— **Cheryl Dellasega, GNP, Ph.D.,**
Associate Professor of Medicine & Humanities,
Penn State College of Medicine-The Milton S. Hershey
Medical Center; author of *Surviving Ophelia*

"Jessica is the single most courageous person that I know. Her book represents a breakthrough in personal honesty and integrity. As a doctor and healer who has successfully treated many diseases considered incurable, the process can be distilled by a single phrase—the essence of healing is finding yourself. In a decade of experience with natural medicine and healing, I have never seen a more authentic work, or worked with a more authentic person. Jessica represents the next major step in the process of healing ourselves. Although the details may differ, you will recognize yourself in this book, or you will recognize a part of yourself that you need to reclaim. If you are on a journey of healing, or would like to be, this book will be of great value to you."

— **Steve Nenninger, M.D.**, Manhattan

"This book is positioned to change the way we think critically about, and respond actively to, social issues that directly impact the lives of women and men everywhere. Jessica Weiner seamlessly fuses autobiography, tales from the field, and strategies for empowerment and, in doing so, challenges us to rethink our lives, our bodies, and our place in a society still so desperately in need of change.

"Students of all ages and in all fields of study will find themselves somewhere in this book. Jessica doesn't simply tell her own story. She gives voice to the lives and experiences of women and men throughout the country who are yearning for better tools for empowering themselves and those around them. Readers are left with a sense of direction, hope, and passion and are given clear strategies for activism and social change, both in their own lives and in the world around them."

— **Brian R. Jara,** Women's Studies Program, Penn State University

A VERY HUNGRY GIRL

A VERY HUNGRY GIRL

How I Filled Up on Life . . . and How You Can, Too!

jessica weiner

HAY HOUSE, INC.
Carlsbad, California
London • Sydney • Johannesburg
Vancouver • Hong Kong

Published and distributed in the United States by: Hay House, Inc., P.O. Box 5100, Carls-bad, CA 92018-5100 • *Phone:* (760) 431-7695 or (800) 654-5126 • *Fax:* (760) 431-6948 or (800) 650-5115 • www.hayhouse.com • **Published and distributed in Australia by:** Hay House Australia Ltd., 18/36 Ralph St., Alexandria NSW 2015 • *Phone:* 612-9669-4299 • *Fax:* 612-9669-4144 • www.hayhouse.com.au • **Published and distributed in the United Kingdom by:** Hay House UK, Ltd. • Unit 202, Canalot Studios • 222 Kensal Rd., London W10 5BN • *Phone:* 44-20-8962-1230 • *Fax:* 44-20-8962-1239 • www.hayhouse.co.uk • **Published and distributed in the Republic of South Africa by:** Hay House SA (Pty), Ltd., P.O. Box 990, Witkoppen 2068 • *Phone/Fax:* 2711-7012233 • orders@psdprom.co.za • **Distributed in Canada by:** Raincoast • 9050 Shaughnessy St., Vancouver, B.C. V6P 6E5 • *Phone:* (604) 323-7100 • *Fax:* (604) 323-2600

Editorial Supervision: Jill Kramer   *Design:* Tricia Breidenthal

Library of Congress Cataloging-in-Publication Data

Weiner, Jessica, 1973-
    A very hungry girl : how I filled up on life and how you can, too! / by Jessica Weiner.
    p. cm.
ISBN 1-4019-0223-5 (Tradepaper)
    1. Weiner, Jessica, 1973—Health. 2. Eating disorders—Patients—United
States–Biography. I. Title.
RC552.E18W445 2003
    362.1'968526'0092—dc21

2003005988

ISBN 1-4019-0223-5

06 05 04 03   7 6 5 4
1st printing, September 2003
4th printing, November 2003

Printed in the United States of America

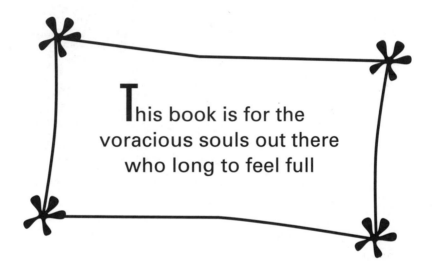

This book is for the voracious souls out there who long to feel full

contents

(**Please note:** While the stories and experiences in this book are based in truth, some of the names have been changed to protect the privacy of the individuals mentioned.)

preface

When I was a little girl, my grandfather would always say, "Jessie, don't forget to write it down!" but I never knew what he meant. I didn't particularly enjoy writing, and I wasn't yet an author at age ten. I was just me—a creative, drama-loving little girl who would rather sing, dance, and watch TV than sit with a notebook and write. I'd imagine entire pop operas for my Barbies to sing, completely improvising the lyrics based on the music of some Broadway hit. I created plays in my head, magical stories of princesses and heroes, evil enemies and unrequited love. In my preteen years, I recruited my sister to participate in these fantasies, and she often had to play the villain. She willingly went along with whatever soap opera I cooked up . . . of course, she had no choice—such is the role of a little sister. But no matter what I imagined, I rarely had a written text to document my adventures.

Whenever I told these tales to my grandfather, he always asked if I'd written them down. Oftentimes I'd answer yes—I'd lie to him and hope that he wouldn't ask me again. I truly didn't know where he was coming from and probably wrote him off as just being an old man. Yet I knew my grandfather loved me and saw me as no one else did. He fed my adventures of the mind and encouraged me to continue pushing the envelope of my creative spirit. Nothing was ever "too much" or "not realistic" for him. Some far-out story was always greeted with a resounding "Yes!" at the top of his lungs, followed by a great hearty laugh that made his belly jump up and down and caused his mouth to reveal his enormous smile full of teeth. My grandpa taught me to play.

In my late teens and even into college, Grandpa would inquire about the classes and projects I was working on, and he'd still ask if I was writing it down. Now my lie had much more substance because technically I was in college and writing down lots of things. I'm sure that none of it was what my grandfather had in mind . . .

or maybe it was. I think he wanted to know if I was recording the life I was living—this beautiful, magical, fantastic journey I was on.

My grandfather certainly marveled at all of my accomplishments and held the door open for me to have many more. Perhaps he imagined that I'd be where I am now—able to look back and record the brilliance of a time passed; to take down the experience, lessons, and knowledge I've gained. Grandpa was a man who loved learning, and well into his later years still took advantage of opportunities and outings that challenged his world and his perspective. He loved living life.

Up until my grandfather died, every time I told him of a new adventure in school, romance, or career, he'd say, "Jessie, don't forget to write it down." And yet I never would. Was it some sort of rebellion, this continual refusal to accept good advice from a family member? Or was there some deeper soul connection—some premonition about my life that he was able to recognize?

I finally began "writing it down" when I decided to face my eating disorder. When I look back on the almost 80 journals I've kept since I was 18, I can't count the number of pages that say, "Why am I writing this? What am I doing?" Yet I wrote. I wrote of my pain. My passion. My struggle. My triumph. As my recovery led me to a career of reaching out, I then wrote of others' pain. Of others' language. Of others' successes. And I recorded the life I was living, observing, and experiencing through my work out in the world. I began to capture other people's stories, too, just in case *they* weren't writing them down.

When I get ready to write something now, I almost go through an actual birthing process: I feel abdominal pain, and I get quite emotional. I cry—a lot. I feel deeply in my entire body, and my brain tingles with what's about to be released. It's the most organic experience I know. I feel close to God and not of this earth—something deeper takes over and guides me to release the "child" (my idea) and let it out in the world. Sometimes the delivery is painful, and sometimes it's so easy that I wonder why I waited so long to try it.

Giving birth to this book has been incredibly difficult, and I've resisted it every step of the way. For years, audience members have asked me after my shows if I had a book they could read. Thousands of people have sought an extension of my work through my words: Mothers begged me to write a book so that they might use it as a guide with their teenage children; college-age women wanted me to write a book about empowerment and overcoming obstacles in order to live a healthy life; men asked me to write a book about women (ha!); and fathers pleaded with me to write a book so that they might better understand why their young daughters starve themselves to death.

I refused. And I lied, like I did to Grandpa. "Yes, I'm writing a book; you can look for it next year," I'd say. Or, "I'm working on that book right now—it'll be out soon." Yet with each falsehood, I felt the urgency to return to my room and begin writing so that I could make good on what I'd promised.

As I mentioned, I always keep my journals, so I was able to refer to the ones I kept during the six years I spent traveling across the country speaking with people and performing; as well as the ones from the five years before that, when I lived and worked through my discomfort with my life and my own illness. I'd recorded all of this not knowing who my audience would be—and even when I had an audience, I still wasn't sure what I'd share with them. But now I do.

This book is broken down into three parts. Part I is my journey of recovering, thriving, and surviving from an eating disorder and the low self-esteem that controlled my life. My journey from an actor to playwright, director, businesswomen, producer, speaker, and now television personality. My journey from dreamer to doer, from child to adult, from woman to healer. My journey of listening to you, hearing you cry, watching you smile, and seeing you make great changes in your life. I'm not a doctor, a therapist, or a clinician—I'm a 29-year-old woman who's living her life and bearing full witness to its delicious twists and turns. I've lived what I write, and I write only my truth.

In Part II, I share the stories from my years on the road. Many of you have trusted me with your emotions and deepest secrets, and I've recorded these moments. Like you, I'm a woman in process, in *progress,* in discovery of what I'm to do on this earth with my precious time. I'm a sister, a daughter, a lover, a best friend, a cousin, a granddaughter, a mentor, a cheerleader, a student, an activist, a soul searcher, a boss, an employee, a communicator, a stranger, an ear, a hug, and a participant in every moment I create. I've created stories that illuminate a larger discussion, and I've watched miracles happen. I've seen transition, hope, love, and triumph and swallowed despair, failure, and hatred—and you'll see it as well in this part of the book.

In Part III, I leave with you some take-away tools and thoughts to continue the process—in other words, suggestions for action and ways to mobilize everyday change.

But before I get to the body of the book, I'd like to introduce you to some special friends of mine—A.G., Rose, and Terri—whose personal experiences, which I call "In Your Voice," represent what I encounter each and every day. As you read this section, perhaps you'll realize that the stories in *A Very Hungry Girl* are yours as well as mine. To honor A.G., Rose, Terri, and every single one of us, I've chosen to write these incredible things down.

May you find what you need in this book—strength, courage, and wisdom. A sense that you're not alone. That great things are indeed possible. That you're worth it. That we survive. That there's a lot for us to do in this world. And that in every bit of language we utter to ourselves and to each other, there's always a message. Choose to make it a message of love . . . and peace.

Grandpa, this is for you. For knowing that I needed to write it down.

And for you, Jessie, for finally doing it.

✳ ✳ ✳

acknowledgments

With gratitude to:

Meekie, Deekie, and Beekie—ILYMTTYAMLTT. It is because of you that I can do this!

The Marcus, Kassab, and Weiner family—what a glorious family to belong to.

Grandma Mollie and Grandpa Michael, who are dancing in heaven.

Grandma Leona, who is *kvelling;* and Grandpa Philip, who is missing her so much.

John Edward, for believing in me and seeing this book.

Ramey Warren Black and Adora English, for loving me and holding the big vision.

My Media-Savvy family, for making dreams come true.

Miagi, for being the first one and always speaking the truth.

Adam Kolbrenner, for driving me nuts while keeping me on target.

Eric Weissler, for being the optimistic pessimist.

Debra Goldfarb, for reading my late-night e-mails.

Danny Levin and Reid Tracy, for encouraging me to be authentic and share my voice.

The Hay House angels: Jill and Shannon for belief, guidance, and serial commas; and Tonya, Amy, Christy, Chandra, and Jacqui for cheerleading and vision.

My dear friends Andre Hudson, Paul Thorpe, Michael Medico, Cory Moore, Carl Pope, Tammi Ramsey, Kristin Richardson, Damone Roberts, Sharon Newport, Lee Zamir, Brady McKay, Doron Silverman, Chris MacEwan, Jamie Gannon, Daysun Perkins, and Jeret Creed for teaching me friendship and showering me with support and love.

Steve and Roseanne Nenninger, for changing and saving my life.

Ettus Media for teaching me to trust.

Denice and Jean Squire, for planting the seeds of strength and clarity.

Bettie Griffin, who always knew.

My Aloha gang, for the "splendids" and remote office space.

Angie McKnight and my babies, for letting me be a part of your family.

To Brian, Marla, and Jill at PSU, thanks for getting it out there.

All the members of A.C.T. OUT Ensemble, for going on this journey with me.

Crazy Hair, for years of friendship, love, and memories.

My girls and a guy—Allison Gerthoffer, Terri Porter, Marni Kahn, Katie Browning, Cari Smulyan, Katie Johnson, and Brady Sharp—the future looks bright with you leading the way.

For every single brave soul who spoke up after a show, or wrote a letter, or called to share your story—your humanity and spirit is what drives me to do this work. God bless you.

✳ ✳ ✳

A Survivor's Story

Three years ago, my life took an interesting turn. I used to call it "a turn for the worse," but I don't think that way anymore. You see, I was violently raped during my junior year of high school, on the day after my 16th birthday. I had voluntarily taken drugs that night—and I was so ashamed that I kept what happened to myself. I didn't even tell my parents because I couldn't bear to think that they might blame me for it because of the drugs. For three years I kept the incident bottled up inside, thinking that if I pretended that it never happened, it couldn't hurt me. I was wrong—it *did* hurt me. It affected my life in ways I never thought possible.

One day my boyfriend came back from a Greek leadership conference with a business card in his hand. He explained that he'd attended a talk on rape and sexual assault and had told the woman speaking that her speech had really hit home because his girlfriend had been raped and wasn't dealing well with it. He was absolutely right. I had reached a point in my life where I couldn't ignore my feelings anymore, and the rape was constantly on my mind. Anyway, I looked closer at the business card he'd handed me. "Jessica Weiner," the name on the card, had told my boyfriend to have me e-mail her if I ever needed to talk to anyone.

For about a week, my boyfriend urged me to contact Jessica. Finally I gave in because I figured that I had nothing to lose—if I didn't like talking to her via e-mail, I could just stop. The first time I wrote her, I was so scared. I didn't like opening up to a complete stranger about my problems. However, as the months progressed, I felt really comfortable talking to Jessica. She's taught me so much.

Jessica was the only person I'd ever really opened up to about my attack, and she never judged me—not once. She made me realize that being raped wasn't something I should be ashamed of. It wasn't my fault, yet by keeping quiet about my assault, I was letting my attacker have power over me. She was right—even though I had no idea who this man was, he'd taken over my life for three years. Jessica showed me that being raped wasn't something horrible that happened *to me,* it was just something that happened. Now I have a completely new outlook on life. I'm no longer the careless teenager I once was—I've matured into a woman with hopes, desires, and dreams that cannot be shattered by anyone, no matter what.

I helped bring Jessica to my college to speak. With her help, I decided that I'd get up and tell my story of being raped. I was incredibly nervous about the event, as it was the first time I'd ever really spoken about what had happened to me. I don't think I could have done it alone; having Jessica there to support me was such a huge comfort. She convinced me that these people cared about me and that I'd really make an impact that night. I was still a little sick to my stomach, but I felt safe because I had her right next to me the whole time. I trusted that she wouldn't let anything bad happen to me.

Jessica and I sat in the front of the room as I proceeded to tell the group my story. I looked around the crowd, paralyzed with shock, and strangely enough, for the first time I felt okay about what had happened to me. I knew that behind some of those surprised faces were people just like me, and maybe I'd inspired someone to seek help for themselves or a loved one. Also, by telling my story I felt as if a huge weight had been lifted from my shoulders. I don't feel like I have to hide anything anymore. What happened to me was a blessing in disguise—if it hadn't happened, who knows where I'd be right now? Who's to say I wouldn't still be doing drugs? I'm very happy with the woman I've become.

My experiences have taught me so much, but I don't think I could have realized anything good about my situation without Jessica. She's amazing at what she does; she truly has a gift.

The empowering message that Jessica sends is unique and absolutely incredible. I'd definitely recommend that women *and* men alike take an interest in her work. She made me feel great about myself at a time when I thought I could never like myself again. If she can get through to me—the most hard-headed, stubborn person in the world—then she can get through to anyone.

To the readers of this book, you're in for such a treat. Jessica's great at sending a profound message without overworking your emotions. She's very funny and down-to-earth; but most important, she'll teach you to love and respect yourself in any situation. She made me realize what really matters in life, and I'm positive that she can do the same for you. She'll show you that you don't need to fit any mold society forms for you—just be yourself and feel good about it. Where she obtained this knack for helping people, I'll never know. What I *do* know is that Jessica Weiner can show you a different, happier, healthier side of yourself. She truly is an angel in disguise.

— **A. G.,** Pittsburgh, PA

A Mother's Words

I recall the enthusiasm in the voices of the people who first told me about Jessica Weiner and her message. As a parent and mental-health worker, I know too well how body-image and self-esteem problems plague our children today. I was totally convinced that it would be well worth the effort to bring Jessica to my daughters' school. After months of anticipation, Jessica indeed delivered a thought-provoking body-image program that captured the audiences of adults and children alike. With great knowledge, passion, and sensitivity, she uniquely shed light on a subject that isn't often understood. She was able to skillfully spark interest in the children who were listening to her, thus increasing the likelihood of impacting them emotionally.

A   V   E   R   Y   H   U   N   G   R   Y   G   I   R   L

Jessica's ability to provide parents and influential adults with invaluable insight into this emotionally destructive subject was key in giving them a sense of understanding and direction as well. As she spoke openly of her own journey, anyone with similar struggles could only be left with feelings of comfort and hope. Getting her message out is a big part of what Jessica Weiner does. More important, how she does it is what makes her who she truly is.

My encounter with Jessica didn't end after the presentation—instead, my daughters and I have had the privilege of developing a special friendship with her. Jessica continues to show interest in my daughters' lives and has remained in contact with them over the last few years through e-mails and phone calls. The fun-loving bond she's created between them has given my daughters a role model who, by example, has shown them self-acceptance and love. I've witnessed Jessica's giving heart and spirit as she travels along her road to educating people. Her compassion goes beyond teaching what she knows and has experienced—she's absolutely dedicated to positively impacting people's lives by showing them the power of human goodness.

Oftentimes our drive to help and understand our children leaves us feeling frustrated and helpless. By writing this book, Jessica provides parents with a valuable and empowering tool that will get us on the road to awareness, knowledge, and action. With her expertise and wisdom, she also gives us direction and hope as we attempt to understand the complex and sometimes devastating relationship between self-esteem and body image. Jessica is an inspiration, and a person whose life's main goal is to make a difference. She definitely has in *our* lives!

— **Rose Cirino Nelson** (Alicia and Kristen's Mom), Erie, PA

xx

An Unexpected Friend

There I was—sitting in the dimly lit corner booth of the smallest (yet most authentic) Mexican restaurant in town, spilling my heart to a complete stranger. We had a conversation similar to what I imagine long-lost siblings have, as we discussed our experiences, feelings, and aspirations. It was the beginning of a friendship with a person I was always looking for but never expected to find—Jessica Weiner, who came to speak at my university and subsequently became my role model, confidante, and friend.

Jessica visited our campus to touch upon the very delicate subject of eating disorders. Through candid conversation, an open heart, and an honest message, Jessica shed light on the source and symptoms of eating disorders in both young men and women. The impact of her discussion and presentation increased awareness, and initiated a renewed sense of responsibility in women to help each other and themselves. Campus leaders such as myself have a responsibility to our peers (and to ourselves) to call on people such as Jessica to address ideas and concepts previously ignored or downplayed by society. We have the unique opportunity to create an environment open to discussion, growth, and change. The feedback from Jessica's appearances is testimony enough to her talent. Before now, young women of the millennial generation—the generation right after the infamous X—haven't had a spokesperson to raise awareness about the issues we face. We're a generation that's been overlooked as too capricious (at least according to the media and pop culture). Consequently, we have mothers, older sisters, and women twice our age offering us advice on topics that were never discussed when they were young.

Jessica addresses the heart of issues all young women and men face *today,* because she's lived through them right along with us. She doesn't offer a secret formula or magic potion; her words are more like those of a good friend—straight from the heart. Jessica's style and message are groundbreaking, and she delivers answers and advice that anyone can relate to. Whether you're coping with an eating disorder (or any other issue) or there's a young woman you care about in your life, Jessica will speak to you.

As one of the most successful, educated, and informed generations of women to ever enter adulthood, it's time that we begin to speak out, and motivate each other to live the most healthy, prosperous, happy lives we can. This book will open a doorway into the minds, hearts, and feelings of today's young people.

— **Terri Porter**, Panhellenic President,
University of Florida

✳ ✳ ✳

part I

THE
INNER HUNGER

chapter 1

Touching Thighs
and the Facts of Life

To help you understand the work I do, I should first explain a little about myself. Or, rather, who I was, what I went through, and how it affects who I'm becoming. Because we're all in process and none of us are complete, I believe that we have a chance at every turn to make a new decision and release old patterns that no longer serve us. We all have those defining moments that impart life lessons for us to remember, but it's what we choose to do with the knowledge gained from those lessons that creates our life's journey. Everyone's path looks different—yet so often we hold ours up against another's to measure and compare. I know that for a long time I felt as if I didn't have a story worth telling or the correct language to express what was going on inside of me.

I never looked like anyone else. I had rich, caramel-colored skin; gigantic brown eyes; and hair that had a curly mind of its own—yet my uniqueness was lost on me, for I wanted to be tall, thin, and blonde. When I was 11 years old, I'd pray extra hard that when I woke up in the morning I'd look like Barbie. Every morning I was disappointed.

I sprouted curves earlier than most of my friends. I remember being in the fourth grade and discovering that my chest had grown these two tiny lumps where it used to be soft and flat. I was mortified. Only one other girl had a bra in my fourth-grade class, and you couldn't tell if it was her boobs or her blubber—but people made sure that she was picked on nonetheless. I feared that my new Kmart bra would be discovered and become fodder for the ridiculous boys in my class. I wanted to be noticed because I looked like a little doll, not because I was some fleshy, awkward, developing geek.

Even my teeth disobeyed me. Don't ask me why, but braces were actually coveted in my elementary school, and retainers were considered cool to wear. Once I actually straightened out a paper clip and stuck it to my front teeth to see what I might look like when I finally got a retainer. Going to the orthodontist was a rite of passage. However, my teeth had spaces in between them, and the two front ones were huge. And to make it worse, not all of my adult teeth had come in yet. I was an early bloomer in the breasts and a late bloomer in the teeth. I never seemed to be in sync. (Only later would I realize that this is called *puberty*.)

I suppose that my dissatisfaction with my body and appearance wasn't unheard of, but at the time I didn't see other girls hate themselves and their appearance like I hated mine. While I was never chubby, I was always soft. My thighs rubbed together when they touched, which was devastation from the start. Later in life, I became obsessed with this fact, carefully noticing the size and shape of thighs around me and the proximity of how close the skin came together. It became a sick distraction and measurement of body ideal. I'd rail against my touching thighs and hold the bulges of flesh in my hands as I raised and lifted my skin apart to see what I might look like with distance between my legs. I'd search through baby photos to see if there was ever a point where my thighs didn't rub together when I walked. Not even as an infant was that the case—in all of those pictures, my thighs still held on to each other. It was just never meant to be. . . .

Katherine St. Claire's thighs didn't touch. When *she* walked, you could actually see space between her thighs. And she always had the newest Jordache or Sergio Valente jeans to accentuate her long legs and hug her tiny waist. She looked like a Barbie doll—tall and lean and every 11-year-old's idol (well, at least mine). She was also mean, which meant that someday I'd be destroyed by her. Naturally, we became friends.

Never did Katherine appear messy or scattered. Her hand-writing was the best in the class, and she had the right combination of smarts and looks to become the teacher's pet. But where I envied her most was in the way boys would talk about her. When I was in school, we weren't nearly as advanced as 11-year-olds are today, but the idea of sex wasn't lost on us either. The cutest boys in our class liked Katherine, and she did what every elementary school hottie did—she remained untouchable and unavailable. She never paired with one guy, which made her all the more desirable.

Now, in all fairness, I'm not sure how aware Katherine was of her looks and what they meant in the ultimate pecking order of grade school. Yet she displayed a sense of entitlement about her status—perhaps she'd never known any other kind of social place-ment. Regardless, she was lucky not to be awkward at that age. For those of us who weren't so lucky, I tell a tale we all can relate to, of not feeling comfortable in your own skin and always wanting to be someone else.

My school certainly had its share of kids to whom adolescence was quite cruel. They had either a disastrously out-of-date wardrobe or socially suicidal traits such as buckteeth, a stutter, bad breath, and excess saliva that shot out of their mouth when they talked—or a combination of all of the above. Unfortunately, when we're young, we're divided right away into the appropriate groups with other people like us. And they provide comfort and safety. Those who aspire to cross over into more popular groups often spend their years wanting to be anything but who they are and no doubt feel a lot of misery.

I spent most of my early years always flirting with the popular groups but never quite landing at their table. I was smart and very verbal in class, and I was accepted on some levels by just about everyone. I didn't have it as rough as some kids did, and I was aware of that luck. And my heart broke for them each time they were knocked down or humiliated in front of the class. I was also grateful that it wasn't me. That attitude alone—the mantra of "Please oh please let them not pick on me"—is what rules elementary school and junior high. This is what keeps us quiet when we know we should tell, it's what makes us keep dark secrets, and it's what causes us to eventually lash out in complete rage.

My creativity kept me happy in class, and I loved expressing myself in artistic ways. I had teachers who encouraged that expression, so I soon soared within the academic world. That helped take my mind off of the awkwardness of not quite being "in" and not quite being "out." I tried my best to blend in, but I secretly wished that I'd just find my niche.

I discovered my heroes and role models on TV. One of my favorite shows was the estrogen-laden *The Facts of Life*. Housemother Mrs. Garrett helped to navigate the very different lives of four girls through the most tumultuous times of their lives—adolescence. There was the fat girl, Natalie, who was funny and strong and a good friend to her brace-faced pal, Tootie. Then there was Blair, who embodied all the things I hated at the time: blonde, pretty, and self-absorbed. But out of all the characters on *The Facts of Life,* I worshiped Jo because she had dark hair and wasn't as thin as a stick. Plus, she said everything that I wanted to say, resisted the ditzy-girl stereotype that Blair seemed to inhabit, didn't wear a lot of makeup, and wasn't always worried if boys thought she was pretty. Jo was tough but sensitive; there certainly weren't many female characters like that on TV at the time. What I admired most was that she got to tell off Blair, my version of Katherine, on a regular basis. I loved that.

I also devoured *ABC Afterschool Specials,* especially anything that featured storylines where the underdog wins against all odds and sweeps the most popular girl/boy off their feet while maintaining their individuality. (Mind you, these themes would go on to permeate all those great John Hughes movies in the '80s.) My absolute favorite special was when the "nontraditional-looking" female (read: curvy, dark hair, not the best dresser) got screwed over by all the popular girls who had become friends with her on a dare, and then she found retribution by having the most eligible jock in school fall madly in love with her for just being . . . herself! *After-school Specials* actually addressed the social hierarchy of school, peer pressure, and young love; and they offered a voice that wasn't my parents' and wasn't my peers'. It was a voice from beyond, from a survivor, someone else going through the exact same things and sharing their story in my language. I would model this voice later on in my work.

Surviving "Weiner" and Broken Birthday Parties

Jane and Michael Weiner, my mother and father, are amazing people. Each time I faced a dilemma, they let me discover the best way to handle it—with just the right amount of help. One of the biggest lessons I learned growing up came on the day of my 11th birthday. I was having a boy/girl party at our house in Miami, Florida, and practically my entire sixth-grade class was invited. At the time I was hanging out a lot with Katherine and her other "doll" friends. I managed to let them talk me into inviting some kids from the junior high school. A girl named Alex, whom I didn't particularly like and everyone was afraid of, was coming to my party, and that somehow made me cool.

Fast-forward to the party. For the first part of the night things went well, and everyone seemed to be enjoying endless pizza and candy and watching movies on TV. Most times at birthday parties you see too much of parents, yet mine were in their bedroom with the door closed that night, and they promised to stay there as long as we behaved ourselves.

The kids had just finished singing "Happy Birthday" to me, when Alex and a few of her pals from junior high arrived. They didn't wish me happy birthday or even anything close to that—they just came in and started eating and bossing people around. Katherine, my supposed friend, and her cronies laughed and egged Alex on. Within minutes they had organized a game of spin the bottle, involving the entire group. Most people played the game and kissed awkwardly, but there was a large group of kids that felt really uncomfortable. And I knew that—after all, I was one of them. I realized that a hurricane of bad kids had just wrecked my party.

There comes a time when you're faced with the decision to take a stand and do something that might not be admired by most. When you're an adult, it's hard enough to do, but when you're a kid, it can be the social kiss of death. My friends Trevor and Jenny, who were fraternal twins, and Mike escaped spin the bottle and found me in the kitchen. "What are you going to do, Jessie?" they implored.

"I'm going to serve the cake—that might take their minds off the game," I brilliantly replied.

"Most of us don't want to play spin the bottle," Jenny said. "We want to go back to watching movies."

"I know," I responded. "Let me handle it."

Jenny, Trevor, and Mike were by all accounts the truest friends I had, and they would certainly prove that to me as the night went on.

I entered my living room to see Katherine locking lips with Brendon, a boy I'd thought bordered on future husband material. This alone made my stomach turn. Then Alex's friend grabbed me and tried to make me kiss Billy Chang, the kid with chronic halitosis at age 11. Since I was holding the birthday cake, I politely refused, desperately trying to maintain being a good host even as I freaked out.

Before I could put the cake down, Alex kidnaped it and began to flick the candles on the floor. They were no longer lit, but the icing was leaving blue and green spots on the carpet. Her friends, who thought that was hysterical, began chasing her with the cake while threatening to shove it in her face.

Hello! I was having a birthday party here! I kept wondering, *What would Jo do?* I knew that she'd come in with her black leather jacket and bad New York accent, and by just narrowing her eyes, she'd scare Alex to death and make her stop. My daydreams were interrupted by a piece of cake flying by my head and landing on the screen door of my patio—white icing suddenly became spackling for the holes in the black screen. Soon, everyone seemed to join in, and a giant cake fight started up.

Trevor and Jenny suggested that I go tell my parents, but I was in shock. I couldn't believe that within ten minutes my party had been ruined. I hated Katherine for inviting Alex and I hated Alex for being cruel, but I really hated myself for what I did next. I ran up to my parents' bedroom and told them that some kids I didn't invite had come over, taken over the party, made people play kissing games, and were now throwing cake all over the patio. I didn't know what else to do. I felt horrible that my parents trusted me and this is what happened.

My dad responded first and stormed out to see what was going on. My mom said, "Don't worry, we'll take care of it." I told her that I'd asked them to stop, which really wasn't true. I don't think I said anything to Alex—I was so overwhelmed with the bullying and saddened at the dramatic turn my birthday party had taken.

When my parents arrived on the patio, cake was *everywhere,* and most of the patio furniture had been turned over in an attempt to become shields for the partygoers. Most kids were laughing, and some were screaming, but they were all oblivious to the disrespect and destruction they were creating. My dad grabbed the remainder of the cake out of Alex's hand and said, "That's enough!" in a tone of fierce defense I'd never heard him use before.

My mother said, "Okay, listen—we're not going to let you destroy our home. We invited you to a party, and we expect you to respect us and our rules." In hindsight, they were quite eloquent considering how angry they were.

My father, recognizing Alex as a ringleader, turned to her and commanded, "Get out!" And she said nothing. But as she hit the front door, she turned around and gave him the finger while making sure that she slammed the door on the way out. Her friends followed behind her without having to be asked. That left me with most of the sixth-grade class staring at my parents and me.

My mom said, "I'm very upset with what you've done to my daughter and to our house tonight. Those of you who did it know who you are. I want anyone who doesn't think that they can respect our rules and our home to leave now. For those of you who want to stay and continue celebrating Jessie's birthday with us, you can do that."

I thought this was great. There's always that fine line you walk when you're a kid where you want your parents to help . . . but not too much. I was actually proud of how they handled it. It reminded me of the retribution I'd seen in the *Afterschool Specials*. Now, everyone would realize what jerks those kids were, and we could go back to eating and watching movies together, and Brendon would forget that he'd kissed Katherine and somehow like me more because my parents had been so cool and forgiving.

But then something went horribly wrong. A majority of the kids turned to Katherine to see what her reaction was. Such is the motion of most kids—look to the popular ones and then follow suit. Katherine looked to her friend Terry, who had been a key player in the cake-throwing incident, and their own guilt must have taken over because they both started walking toward the door. *What? Where are they going?* I wondered. And just as fast as Hurricane Alex had blown in and ruined the night, now Hurricane Katherine was going to leave the place in further ruins by walking out with almost the entire sixth-grade class.

I watched as one by one, the popular kids filed out after Katherine. Brendon didn't even look at me or say he was sorry. Even the unpopular kids and the ones who were having a great time watching movies walked out. I ran to the door, wanting to beg them not to leave my party, and they were all standing there in my front yard looking pissed off. They had no right to be, since it was *their* actions that had caused this upheaval.

As my parents stood behind me, the image of a group of kids staring at me from the front of my house with hate in their eyes became emblazoned on my brain—and I'd see it repeated for another four years.

Katherine said, "Your party sucked."

And her trash-mouthed counterpart, Terry, said to *my mother,* "Fuck you, you fat bitch." A bunch of kids laughed and some said other things I can't remember. Then they all turned around and left.

I returned to the living room to discover that not everyone had left. Trevor, Jenny, and Mike remained. They were the only kids not afraid of my parents, their words, or their anger. They were truly my friends. They helped us clean up, and we spent the rest of the night putting together a big jigsaw puzzle at the kitchen table. I felt like a geek, a complete loser. So I ended up spending my 11th birthday mortified, in shock, and scared to go to school on Monday.

Being a girl with the last name of *Weiner* is nothing but an exercise in building character. Yes, it *is* pronounced "WEE-ner," like the hot dog, not "WHY-ner" (which I'm not sure would be much better).

There isn't one stupid joke I haven't heard. For example:

"What's your dad's name—"

"Harry?

"Big ol'?"

"Oscar Mayer?"

And for everyone else out there with a funny last name, I can't honestly tell you that the jokes stop when you reach a certain age. Even today when adults hear my last name, many of them giggle and try to throw their hat into the ring and come up with yet another play on words. You have to be tough, strong, and able to laugh it off—there's simply nothing else to do. The fact that I braved school on a daily basis hearing taunts and teases about my last name should have put me into some special category for kids with steely self-esteem, but that wasn't entirely the case. What I became good at was deflecting the comments that came my way, much like Wonder Woman deflecting bullets with her magic bracelets. I became adept at verbal sparring. Fighting with my words. Creating witty comebacks to stupid accusations and insults.

Often my parents coached me in this area. We employed creativity in our problem solving—we'd role-play, and I'd practice what I'd say in response to getting teased. My dad was particularly sympathetic. He should have been—after all, he, too, had lived through the hell of the "Weiner curse."

This verbal warfare would come in handy when I returned to school following my birthday fiasco. I'd watched as everyone in my class had turned their backs and walked out of my party, and that experience was not forgotten Monday morning. The lines were drawn, and I still had only three people on my team—Trevor, Jenny, and Mike.

I must hand it to these little human beings for choosing to be so strong when they could have easily followed the crowd. Pre-teen friendships can sometimes hold within them some very grown-up concepts such as loyalty, character, and conviction. Anyway, that Monday I encountered the typical gossip that accompanies a scandalous event, and getting "kicked out" of my birthday party was the way everyone was choosing to see the incident. I spent some very lonely days waiting out the wrath of the class, until the excitement wore off for most of the kids and they went back to picking on Billy Chang. But Katherine, Terry, and the rest of the "instigators" enjoyed my ostracism—and soon their challenges became physical.

I was invited to fight Terry on the hill behind my school that was the common meeting ground for fighting, especially with girls. Terry, who clearly was the bruiser of her particular crowd (she sported shoulders wider than most boys in our class and could beat most of them at arm wrestling), dared me to kick her ass on a regular basis. I found it funny how Terry somehow escaped being picked on for her less-than-skinny body and not-so-good looks.

At home, I'd tell my mother about Terry's taunts, oftentimes leaving out the physical threats—not because I didn't want my mom to worry but mostly because I had no intention whatsoever of letting Terry kick my butt. I was a pretty passive kid, but I wasn't going to allow myself to be scared off by a loud-mouthed girl who I knew had a troubled home life. Terry's mom slapped her on a regular basis, and I'd even witnessed it once at her own birthday party. I was sensitive to what Terry must have been going through at home, but that still didn't give her a right to unleash her pain on me. I wasn't so much as scared of Terry as I was just frustrated that I had to endure this conflict in my social life—her veiled threat of violence was more of an inconvenience and an embarrassment than an actual cause for alarm. It was 1984—you can tell that I went to school years before Columbine.

My mother was so cool. Her best comeback was, "You tell Terry when she says something to you that she's so low you can't even touch her with a ten-foot pole." It was corny, but it worked. I said it to Terry after English class, and it drove her nuts.

"Then if she really gets up in your face," Mom advised, "ignore her. Look right through her, or better yet, just walk on by—and *smile*."

She was right again. This defense really irked Terry and Katherine, and slowly they got the message that I couldn't be ruffled anymore. Their constant harassment died down a bit, but there was always a simmering tension between the three of us. They didn't trust me, and I certainly didn't trust them. In fact, my faith and trust in people my own age was seriously tested during that year. I saw the weakness of my classmates, and I gained a new respect for my own strength in not succumbing to the pressure to fight back on their level. I also had so much admiration for Trevor, Jenny, and Mike, who never really understood what staying behind with me at my party meant in the long-term message of friendship.

Unfortunately, I had no idea what was to come in the following years of junior high school and how Terry, Katherine, Brendon, and many nameless, faceless others would come back to teach me more lessons—this time about restraint, pride, and dignity.

Despite a disastrous birthday party, my sixth-grade year brought me a fabulous opportunity to audition for a performing-arts junior high school way out of my local district in another part of Miami. This wonderful program housed actors, dancers, musicians, and artists; if selected, I'd take a half day of theater classes on top of my normal academic requirements. I was very excited about this opportunity—not only would it mean that I could escape these neighborhood kids, but my local junior high was rumored to have become overpopulated and riddled with drugs and apathetic, outnumbered teachers. I could pursue the one thing that was keeping me sane as a child: drama.

If there was ever a saving grace in my life (besides my family), it was my love of the arts. The world of imagination and creation held a space for me where I was free to laugh, play, and explore all things magical. Yet fantasy and make-believe alone didn't do it for me. Even as a young girl I was drawn to plays or movies with social messages, just outcomes, and moral lessons. I related to the struggle to achieve something you fought hard for. I savored characters that overcame hardships to eventually enjoy victory, success, and long-lost love. There was a deep romantic side to me—even at age 11, I found myself attracted to anything with a love story. The complicated relationships between men and women were something I actually looked forward to—I couldn't wait to be in love, win big, and feel success. Drama and creating offered me an escape from my uncomfortable world, but it also gave me hope that I could rewrite any situation I found myself in.

Being that I loved language so much, which was a gift from my grandfather, I became a good actor. Words held power for me—I savored the way they fell out of my mouth, and I enjoyed the way I could manipulate them to tell a story. I was outgoing and bold in my acting. Taking risks on the stage thrilled me.

In the fifth grade, my teacher, Mrs. Stormer, allowed me to experiment with words in her English class. We were learning about adjectives and were going over the usual list of suspects: *big, fat, blue* . . . when she issued a challenge: "I want you to take this list of adjectives and create a story around them. You only have to use one or two adjectives, but I want you to come back tomorrow and share your story."

I returned the next day having used all 12 adjectives we'd discussed in a story about the *big, fat* lady in the *ugly blue* dress. When Mrs. Stormer called on me to read my homework assignment, something came over me, and an accent flew out of my mouth—the origin of which I'm not quite sure, but it sounded funny and it made people laugh. In fact, the entire English class was cracking up, and I fell more in love with performing than ever before. But better than that, they were laughing at what I wrote, what I'd created, and the power to move them with my words had me hooked.

Mrs. Stormer, sensing that a big drama queen had been born, allowed me to come in each week and read my stories. And even though we'd finished the chapter on adjectives, I got extra credit and months of storytelling experience. Better yet, I built an identity around something I did well. Acting, writing, and performing all became friends to me . . . and I needed them.

My parents weren't actors, but they knew instinctively how to nurture my creativity and never once discouraged my acting pursuits, not even when I chose to major in it in college. I never had that talk with my father where he tried to tell me that only 2 percent of actors make a living at it; instead, we conversed as if he always knew I'd *be* in that 2 percent. My mother also got behind my passion tenfold and enrolled me in drama and dance classes. It was there that I began preparing for the audition that would set the rest of my life in motion.

I used the final talent show of my sixth-grade year to showcase a monologue I planned to use as my audition piece for Southwood, the performing-arts junior high. The piece had to do with being picked on in school, and how one young child's pain turned him into a bully. I didn't write it, although I could have—I chose it because it represented what was going on in my life. This piece also demonstrated my ability to read an audience and know what they wanted. I won the talent show, beating out Katherine and Terry's modern-dance version of Billy Joel's "Uptown Girl." For me, that win couldn't have been sweeter.

When it came time to audition at Southwood, I almost didn't come out of the stairwell, where I'd holed up with my mother. I kept telling her I was too scared to go in and do my monologue. I wanted to get into this school with all my heart, yet I was petrified of failing. Taking this risk presented a huge challenge to my self-esteem, and on the day of my audition I almost let the negative voices of Katherine and Terry in my head distract me and sabotage my performance.

My mother not-so-gently said, "Okay, Jessie, if you don't want to do it, then let's go home." She picked up her keys and exited the stairwell, and I decided on the spot to go the other way and wander into the auditorium, where the audition orientation was being held. Once I got up onstage and did my piece, all negative voices floated away, and I had a ball. And a few months later, after repeatedly chasing down the mail carrier to see if my letter came, I was accepted to Southwood.

News spread throughout my class that I wouldn't be going on to junior high with everyone else. For some reason, that made Katherine and Terry furious—perhaps because I was thriving even though I wasn't in their cult, or maybe I seemed happy for the first time all year and satisfied with myself. My new confidence must have shone, because they did a good job of messing it up. That's when they discovered the word *fat* and how it could be used against me as a weapon deadlier and more potent than Terry's fists. This word got inside me and destroyed me at the core. It was a word that meant many different things to me—ugly, undesirable, left out, rejected, and wrong. Once the power of this word was discovered and my weakness exposed, those girls used it against me as often as they could . . . until eventually I took up their battle and used it against myself.

"Fat bitch." I found those words scribbled in a note left in my desk, and I knew who'd left it there. It was the same thing Terry said to my mother when she walked out of my birthday party. But what was worse than the "f" word itself was the bittersweet image it was painting in my head. As I became stronger, clearer, and curvier, I felt uglier, like I was taking up too much space. I didn't recognize Katherine and Terry's attacks as jealousy, inadequacy, or fear that I had a passion. I was off practicing monologues and creating new characters to play, while they were busy buying identical outfits and trying to woo Brendon.

I was delighted about my new school and the fact that I'd gotten accepted, yet whenever I allowed this image of my being undesirable, big, and clumsy to fill the space in my head, my enthusiasm would wane. I started looking at people on television—all of them looked like Katherine, and nobody looked like me. I instantly entered a war between my head and my heart, a war that would rack up many causalities over time . . . the first one being my sense of self.

The Egging Tradition

Southwood offered me a fresh palette from which to paint new friends, experiences, and opportunities, and I savored the fact that no one from my elementary school had followed me there. I was free (for now).

Junior high moved at a faster speed and held within it more complicated relationships and boys, boys, boys! By this time I'd started my period, so my hips had widened considerably since grade school. Almost overnight I could trace the indentation from my waist back out to my hips and then back down to my thighs. I looked more like a violin than a lean rectangle, which is what most of my new friends resembled. For example, there was Josie, a dancer who had the most beautiful long hair I'd ever seen and eyelashes to match. We were in drama classes together, although at the time she was a better dancer than actor. Josie wanted to be on Broadway, and she looked like a delicate porcelain figurine you'd want to protect and nurture. She and I would carry our friendship through high school and on and off into college, and it would be through her that I learned even more why I should hate my body for betraying me with curves. Josie punished hers so severely that by the time we were of driving age, she hadn't started to menstruate yet. Yet she and I connected on a deep level, and her sweetness and love for me was just what I needed.

Josie helped me put together the guest list for my 12th birthday party. I was at a new school with new friends, so I was sure this party was going to be better than last year's. Our main priority was to stock the party with as many boys and as much junk food as possible. You see, we both loved boys, and Josie's mom didn't allow her to eat sugar, so she binged on it whenever she wasn't home.

We got every sweet imaginable to serve at the party—which was fitting, since my birthday is on Halloween. Josie and I also decided to make it a costume party, so we'd all go trick-or-treating and then come back and gorge on our finds while flirting mercilessly with the boys we'd invited, especially Kyle.

Kyle was a delicious blond boy who, at the ripe old age of 12, knew how to woo a girl right out of her training bra. He was smooth and confident and made a really good girlfriend, too, seeing how he wasn't afraid to talk about clothes, makeup, or movies. Little did we know then that these telltale signs meant that Kyle didn't play on our team—a fact he'd realize himself in about 15 years.

Having a birthday on Halloween is wonderful because there's a little added excitement in the air when people dress up. And I was so ready to have a special birthday this year. So a group of us gathered at my house and immediately began to strategize our plan for getting the most candy out of my neighbors. We were about ten strong, since at that age traveling in a pack was the most efficient and preferred method of travel. We were a gaggle comprised of four baby dolls (one of which was me), one hobo, two superheroes, one ballerina (Josie, of course), one cowgirl, and a somewhat drunken-looking clown. We took up most of the street when we walked; and we were loud, goofy, and obnoxious.

Our neighborhood had a few houses notorious for their Halloween getups, so we decided to hit those last. After leaving a house where Josie had managed to talk the person into giving her three extra Snickers bars, we ran into Katherine and a group of her new junior high friends. Whereas my group was predominately female, Katherine's was mostly male (including Brendon) and easily twice the size. She spotted me and words were exchanged. This time, instead of heeding my mother's advice of walking past and smiling, I felt protected by my new friends. Katherine still chose to use her weapon in the form of the word *fat,* but this time I countered with a word of my own—*whore.* And I didn't feel any better for sinking to her level. Soon everyone was involved in a yelling match, each slur becoming more disgusting. One of Katherine's people threw an egg at a girl in our group, barely missing her. Since this situation had turned scary and was no longer exciting, I decided to lead everyone back to my house.

None of my friends really questioned why that group started fighting with me. For some reason, groups of people being rude to each other, and fighting other people's battles and never asking why, was a common occurrence in junior high. It smacked of mob mentality.

Back at my house, I didn't tell my parents about seeing Katherine. My friends counted our loot and gave Josie most of our chocolate. All ten of us were jammed in my room, and I began to open presents. That's when we heard something hit the window. Then we heard it again. Kyle opened my blinds to reveal two long yolky streaks streaming down the outside.

I immediately ran to the front door and looked through the peephole. Outside, a group of kids was lined up on my lawn like an army of nitwits waiting for their orders. My party started to shriek in emotion, some of it excitement at what was going on, some of it the adrenaline that gets stirred up when you're directly involved in conflict. I told them to be quiet so as not to alert my parents. I thought that if we just stayed inside, the angry mob would get bored and go home. No such luck. I heard them saying things involving my last name, daring me to come out from inside the house. Then they said, "Happy Birthday, you fat bitch," and started to hurl eggs at my door. Their cheering, laughing, and hooting only enhanced the attack. My friends ran inside my bedroom to look from my window; meanwhile, my parents had heard the commotion and ran to the front door, where I stood with my eye pressed up against the peephole.

Some eggs hit my dad's car, but mostly they landed on our roof and the lawn. Then my dad opened the door, and they threw eggs at him, too. By the time he'd made it halfway to where they were standing, they'd all scattered like cockroaches. The neighbors came out from their homes, and the lady next door said she'd seen the attack and knew who the kids were. My dad said, "We know who it was, too." He looked destroyed—for me and for him. My mom went outside to help him clean up and instructed me to go back into my party. What party? By now our little group of ten was buzzing from all the excitement and gossiping among themselves. They all left before I finished opening my presents. Another birthday party was ruined, and this time I felt responsible.

"How did this happen, Jessie?" my mother demanded.

"I don't know," I lied. "I saw Katherine and her friends out on the street, and we said things to each other—then the next thing I knew, they were here."

My dad was careful not to direct his anger toward me, since he knew that my birthday had just been interrupted yet again. He just said, "You can't give in to them and let them have power over you. You have to ignore them." Much easier said than done—I was embarrassed, hurt, and very sad.

As time went by and I became more ensconced in my life at Southwood, I lost almost complete contact with anyone from my elementary school. I didn't hear about them or from them unless it was my birthday. For the next three years, I had to endure egg attacks on my home every Halloween night from these kids. My parents and neighbors were now on a mission to prevent the egging from happening each year. And each year they failed. They all sat in their driveways distributing candy—some of our neighbors even parked their cars on the sidewalks to prevent large groups from forming on their front lawns. Still, the gangs came at some point in the night, whether I'd seen or spoken to them or not. I'd even given up trick-or-treating after the first year—now I had parties where we stayed inside the whole night. We couldn't go out and celebrate because we were afraid of what might go on if we left the house. And I had to be careful about the kids I invited over—I almost had to warn them ahead of time that something might happen.

The whole thing was completely humiliating. I made it a point not to instigate or spread rumors or gossip about this group. I was trying to move on, now that I was almost in high school. But it was the worst way to celebrate a birthday—knowing that at some point the night would be ruined and I'd end up feeling powerless. My parents even made pleas to some of the kids' parents and called the police, but they had bigger crimes to handle that night, such as bashed-in mailboxes. "You should be thankful you're not dealing with that," they'd say.

My family had grown so tired and angry from all of this that my dad started sitting outside with a baseball bat. If a kid looked at him funny he was ready—to do what, I don't know, since my father wouldn't hurt anyone. But his family was being threatened, his home vandalized, and his daughter's well-being violated.

By the last year of this "tradition," I think word had spread that this was some sick ritual kids could do to some girl with a funny last name who'd once pissed off the group that Katherine ran. Now it was open season. Around 11:00 P.M., a group started forming, hanging around like they were waiting for someone. Very casually they stood in the street facing our house. My father warned them to move on, and our neighbors threatened to call the police, but they stood there verbally taunting us. (It dawns on me now how unafraid of authority this group was.) This time I stepped outside of my house to look at who was there.

There they gathered on my front lawn, their numbers having grown to upwards of 60 people. I didn't recognize anyone in the crowd, but they were there to hurt me. Cowards. The group was larger than I'd ever seen before. This had definitely become a screwed-up legend at the junior high school.

Before anyone could take out an egg, my father got up from his chair, baseball bat in hand, and stood facing them. I could only imagine what he was going through. My father is one of the sweetest human beings on the planet. He's had to endure tough times himself because of his unwillingness to fulfill male stereotypes. My dad was always athletic-looking on the outside and yet so kind and sensitive on the inside, qualities that women seem to gravitate toward and men seem to punish. Men like my father are not always encouraged by our world. He's not a fighter, but a man with a gentle soul. Yet tonight he was fighting for me and for himself. Someone from the back of the group lobbed an egg that landed on the sidewalk, and that was all it took.

My dad started chasing this group with his baseball bat, and once again they scattered like roaches, only this time my father caught up with one of them by hurling the bat toward his legs. The bat hit the kid, who fell down, then got back up and ran off. In all the commotion, the group had had the chance to throw only one egg, and its gooey mess landed on the sidewalk, not on our house or cars. It was as if someone shot too soon and messed up the whole plan. Although my dad came back with tears in his eyes because he was afraid that he might have hurt someone, I was glad it was over. At least I had hoped it was.

I made it through my next birthday without incident—I was never so relieved in my life. I wanted nothing more than to put those horrible memories behind me. Celebrating my birthday had a weird stigma attached to it for years to come. Even today, I always need to feel safe on my birthday night. And special. It's not hard to understand why. After a while I completely internalized the assaults on my home as a direct attack on my personality, my appearance, and my very existence on Earth. I was ashamed that I was the focus of such a cruel tradition. I felt rage that I never fully expressed, so I turned it inward and began a quest to become as blended and accepted as possible. As tiny as possible, as non-troublemaking as possible. I wanted to take up the least amount of space I could. So I returned to hating my body, where I had more control and could see immediate results. After all, my body was just the outside manifestation of me, and people were throwing eggs at and hating me, weren't they?

On top of all of this, I was now surviving in a competitive-arts program in which teachers thought nothing of telling us how fat or out of shape we were—all under the guise of being "professional." And so, the assaults on my spirit would continue through junior high, only this time the perpetrators would shift from being a gang of insecure preteens to a middle-aged, unhappy teacher named Roy Avery.

A Killer Teacher and Ethel Merman

Roy Avery found his power in being at the center of Southwood's drama program. Parents clamored for their children to be admitted to it; and once inside, the kids kissed Roy's butt to get good parts and even better recommendations to the performing-arts high school. Even though I enjoyed working with other teachers more than Roy, in the end he was the one I was always trying to please, as he was in charge of casting the shows. In competitive-arts programs, the head teacher holds the key to your happiness, or so you're led to believe. Those teachers must use their positions wisely or else they're at risk for murdering the innocence of many children.

Roy was a killer.

There was no doubt that he thought I was talented—he told me so from the moment I auditioned till the moment I graduated. It was what he said and did in between those times that did the most damage. Roy always needed to be in control, and if you were to challenge that, you risked upsetting his whole existence at the school.

I remember we were doing a show where I had a good shot at playing the lead. There was something about the character's life and my own that clicked. Yet I was in a heated callback situation against a girl named Sharon, who was so pert and cute and pretty that she looked like—of all people in the world—Katherine. We were complete opposites, and Roy treated the situation as if either one of us could play that part. I believed in his believing in me, so I went for it and acted my heart out in the audition.

Afterwards, Roy asked to see me. He sat me down on a yellow plastic chair, but his behind was too big to fit in one himself, so he made a joke and sat on the top of the desk that was attached to his chair.

He told me that he had no doubt I was the best one for the role. I got so excited that I'd done a great job of auditioning and nailing the character that I started to smile from the inside out.

Then he decided to kill me. "But you're too ugly to be a leading lady," he said. "You just don't have the looks. You'll always be a little chubby and play Ethel-Merman types."

He'd only just begun.

"You're one of the most talented students I've ever taught," he continued, "but you're not *ingenue* material. It's really too bad that you're not a little thinner, because then I might see you in this role.

23

But I have to give it to Sharon. Anyway, I just wanted you to know that you did a good job."

We were alone in the auditorium, and he had all the power. His body literally sat above mine as he leaned down and almost whispered as he handed me his verdict. I felt hot inside and wanted to leave. I scooted out of the chair and said nothing.

He stopped me, wanting a hug. *Why?* To make amends? To confuse me? To make himself feel better? I didn't know what to do, so I awkwardly turned away, walked out the door, and found myself in front of the school, where my mom was waiting to pick me up. I felt like someone had punched me in the stomach. That wasn't the kind of reaction I was expecting at all. I thought for sure that he was pulling me aside to tell me I got the part and to go over rehearsal schedules. I never would have imagined him saying what he did to me. I knew that getting a part in a play at school was as much about validation as it was about performing, so I absorbed his words and kept them in my arsenal of self-sabotage weapons. I took what he said to heart and blamed my looks for making me lose the part.

I'm sure that millions of performers have felt this way about themselves. They blame their noses, hips, and bellies on missed job opportunities, fame, and fortune. But that really isn't the truth—it's not because of our looks but rather *who's doing the looking*. My worthiness on that day was based on Roy's perception of beauty and what the character should look like. While it's certainly a director's prerogative to hold his or her vision in high regard, it's *not* his or her right to demean an actor or belittle a child. Roy did both. And he did it with such ease, because it was part of his own skewed perception of life. But I wasn't armed with such knowledge then. Instead, his words held the weight of the world for me. Over the next few years, I'd watch him do the same thing to many others. He always gave different hurtful reasons—even though they were his opinions, there are some things that should never be spoken to students in a learning environment. Being told you're too ugly is one of them.

I went on to flourish at the school despite my intense dislike of Roy Avery. I played many funny "Ethel Merman-type" roles, and made the most of my time there. Mr. Avery even ended up giving me the lead in my last school production. I *finally* played a leading lady in *Once Upon a Mattress.* I played Winnifred, a role that hadn't been played by Ethel Merman, but was made famous by Carol Burnett. Nonetheless, she was as non-leading lady as they come. I was able to forget everything while I was onstage and found great comfort in portraying a character that was misunderstood by many until she finally proved to them that she was a princess after all.

At the end of my ninth-grade year, I was accepted to the New World School of the Arts, a new performing-arts high school in downtown Miami. It was modeled after the Fiorello H. LaGuardia School of Music & Art and Performing Arts (the *Fame* school) in New York City. Not everyone in my acting class made it in—Kyle didn't, but Josie did. However, Josie decided to go into dance instead of theater. Roy had also gotten to her and had killed off any hope she might have had that she'd be a great actor. "You'll always be a cute, pretty, little dancer," he told her, "not a serious actress."

Josie added Roy's comments to her own perception that she had to stay cute and tiny to be liked, so sometime in the eighth grade she stopped eating. Another one of our friends had starved herself that year and had gotten lots of attention for it, so Josie followed suit, hoping to remain small and special.

I, too, continued the war against my growing, changing body. I straightened my unruly curls and made them lay down with chemicals. However, my hair had a strong spirit, and the ends rebelled into a curled position reminiscent of Snow White. I finally got braces and couldn't remember why I thought it was such a cool thing in grade school. Now my metal mouth was painful and cut my lips. Plus, I was dying to experience my first kiss, and who in their right mind wanted to kiss a "brace face"?

On the other hand, my breasts had gotten their fair share of attention from boys in junior high, especially Kyle, who reminded me on daily basis how awesome my boobs were. For some reason they were the currency of school culture. Girls who were developed landed in their own category. So now a portion of my body was singled out as being worthy, but I still didn't feel like a whole package. I was nowhere near being comfortable in my own skin. It was like I'd taken the emotional turmoil and social lessons of the past years and ironed them on as patches of self-hatred resting on my thighs, hips, and stomach.

I rallied against my curves and unique appearance. If I heard my mother say one more time that my "exotic looks will be appreciated someday," I thought I'd scream.

When you get a lot of unwanted attention as I had, whether it was from kids at school egging my house or Roy destroying my confidence, you try your best to gain any ounce of control you can over situations. You become your own spin doctor. I discovered that I could create a new form of attention if I came back from a winter or summer break looking thinner than before I'd left. So I made it my mission while I was on vacation to starve myself days before reappearing at school to get the approval I craved. This kicked off a cycle of starving, bingeing, and hating that would follow me into my next adventure—high school.

✳ ✳ ✳

Baked Chicken
and Barfing

I don't remember eating much in high school. Every day became a battle of will and determination against my enemy: hunger. Hunger signified a weakness, a need, and a desire—all of which could be used against me in a game of verbal sparring with my enemies. I tried so hard to avoid hearing the word *fat* associated with my identity that I essentially starved myself for four years. Although there would be periods of gorging, giving in to the hunger and need for nourishment, I spent most times being "not hungry" while trying desperately to ignore the growls from my tummy.

New World School of the Arts was exactly what you would imagine a performing-arts high school to be. Teachers were called by their first names, curse words weren't forbidden, students could wear dance clothes and costumes to class, and instruments and artists' books were commonly found stacked against the wall next to backpacks and headphones. Creativity oozed from the pores of this school, complete with an open campus that allowed us to mingle outside during class, soaking up the atmosphere of hot, sunny downtown Miami.

Our school was housed for a while on the campus of a community college, so we ran amuck with adults and the occasional homeless person. Freedom, art, rebellion, and a strong sense of possibility were our school colors. Since we were artists and just about every second of our time was spent pursuing our craft, we didn't have typical sports teams. Instead, we boasted a multi-grade softball team aptly named "The Fighting Pigeons," as those dirty birds nesting on the outdoor escalators were our true school mascots. And yes, we danced in the streets. As I mentioned before, our school was modeled after the *Fame* school, and in our cheesy attempt to capture the energy of that glorious television show, we danced like fools in the pond outside our science building.

I'd never been around so many talented beings (and so many egos) in my life—and that was just our faculty. The students were an amazing blend of grit, determination, spunk, and pure genius. Each discipline was able to blend with the others, so that afforded me the opportunity to meet other students with gifts.

My friend Josie soon found her home among the dancers. She seemed to fit in and became a popular fixture with the boys. By now we were 16, and Josie still hadn't begun to menstruate. She skipped lunch on most days or opted for the "dancer's delight": a 16-ounce nonfat frozen yogurt. I knew she was starving. I could see it in her eyes.

"What are you doing eating chicken for breakfast?" Josie once asked me in a tone filled with both wonder and disgust.

"I'm on a high-protein diet," I snapped back, pissed off that I had to endure baked chicken at 9 A.M. While others stuffed themselves with bagels and doughnuts, I had to eat a carefully balanced meal of chicken and a large salted cucumber. This routine had helped me lose 6 pounds, which I was hoping would turn into 30.

"You know I've been throwing up, right?" Josie said daringly.

"No," I replied. "Why are you doing that?" I wasn't really sure where this was heading.

"I've been throwing up since we were 12. Remember how I ate all that food at your bat mitzvah, and everyone laughed because I could put away, like, three pieces of cake?"

"Yeah."

"Well, I didn't put it anywhere—I barfed it up. And I've been doing this for a while. I know it's wrong and I have to stop, but I just want to lose a few more pounds for dance."

These words—*for dance*—would soon accompany every rationale for bad behavior that Josie displayed. It became the catchall for the hatred of her body and the unrest within her heart.

I'd continue to share dieting conversations and dialogue about food and weight and how to get rid of it all with a whole host of characters over the next four years, but my talks with Josie about the war she waged with her body would remain our secret for a while.

I first learned about dieting by watching my mother. My best memories of her involve lying on top of her body and just holding on while she kissed and nuzzled my neck. I've always known my mother to be a large woman, so climbing up on top of her for a hug also involved feeling her rolls of flesh and softness envelop me with love. Anyone who meets my mother doesn't soon forget her. She's bold, loud, loving, and fully takes up space, both physically and emotionally. She's also a fierce supporter, a loyal friend, and a passionate mother. And I believe that she's hated her body for most of her life—at least that's what she's told me.

Mom was left alone as a little girl, since my grandmother went to work as a teacher in a time when most women didn't work outside the home. My mother felt abandoned when her mother went to be with "other people's children," so she turned to food as comfort, as solace for her loneliness. Rewards for being "such a brave child" earned my mom extra money that she could use after school, and she'd spend it on sandwiches and cookies. She ate to fill a void—a pattern she continued throughout her adult life. She's just now beginning to untangle the web of overeating that has suffocated her happiness and inner peace.

I remember being in a grocery store with my mother and having another woman peer into our cart and critique our food selections, as if this woman had license to scold and shame us. Sometimes Mom and I talked about such experiences; sometimes we didn't; but at some point in my growing-up years, we began to diet together. I saw the pain on my mother's face when she didn't lose weight after weeks of trying newfangled diets, and I saw her joy when she dropped a dress size or two and felt as if she was on her way to becoming her true self. What she and I didn't know then was that her true being was present all the while, begging us to look at her and recognize her for who she was. . . .

My father has always struggled with his weight, too. For him, the connection between food and control has always been immensely strong. He feels better when he's on a regimented program, and I've spent many nights watching him work out in layers of clothes and trash bags, in an attempt to sweat his stress. He's spent many years on a roller-coaster journey to his true hunger, veering from a strict diet to bingeing with foods his body can't process.

I watched enough of my parents dabbling in the worlds of self-loathing and disordered eating to know that our house was essentially fat-phobic, and I didn't want to be fat. It was that simple. I'd spent most of my preteen years ducking the taunts I was subject to in grade school and the impressions that were made in junior high. It was now time to break free and create a new image.

Eating baked chicken at 5:30 A.M. became normal for me. Sometimes I was so hungry when I woke up that I actually looked forward to it. I ate it again for lunch and sometimes for dinner—in fact, I didn't eat much else. But I thought about it. Constantly. I also thought about Josie's method of "releasing" her meals, but I couldn't do it. Throwing up would mean I was bulimic and had a problem. I didn't have a problem! Except that I ate chicken multiple times during the day and little else. Nope, no problem here!

I'd go to school for seven hours, then go to rehearsal for a few hours, then go home, do homework, and get back up at 5:30 A.M. and do it all over again. I was barely eating 500 calories a day—and soon my body responded to the regime, dropping weight. I was rewarded by getting into the smallest size I could muster, a size 9. Since at various times in my adolescence, I fluctuated from a size

10 to 14, this was quite an accomplishment for me. Now keep in mind that I spent hours a day with dancers and actresses who were maybe a size 1 or even 0. Being a size 9, while it took all the effort I could manage, just seemed light-years away from a size 0. I hated my body for not being smaller. I began measuring my worth by my clothing labels: Smalls made me happy; mediums let me know I needed to be more dedicated to my dieting; larges indicated that I'd slipped up bad and was a worthless cow; and if I had to venture into an extra large, then it was clearly time for a Monday-morning diet.

Our society hates and shames fat people. Making jokes about appearance and weight is the last bastion of acceptable discrimination—I saw that firsthand with my mother. This mind-set doesn't only affect those who are severely overweight; many of us who don't embody the established "norm" feel isolated, discouraged, and defeated. We're set up on this path to attain someone else's body type—and therein lies the trick. It becomes a never-ending journey of destruction that causes us to travel farther away from knowing ourselves. As a teenager, I was already aware of this on many levels, although I didn't have the appropriate language to articulate it. So I found that the perfect way to have power over all of the out-of-control feelings and experiences in my life would be to watch what I ate, deny myself nourishment, and secretly wish to disappear.

High school is a hotbed for the turbulent adolescent lessons of identity, courage, and self. Hormones are in full swing, bodies are changing and flowering, and the pecking order of teenage popularity intensifies. At my school, we had all of that and the added temperament of artists, many of whom used their bodies as the main instrument in their craft. The actors in my program expressed their rebellion and experimentation through drugs and sexuality. Either they spent time getting high, getting laid, or trying to do both. For many reasons, I didn't gravitate toward this expression. When you're not feeding your body, you're certainly not tapped in to its sexual needs; and while I continued to be a full-fledged romantic, sharing my body with another person scared me. My body wasn't ready yet—it was still under construction . . . 23 more pounds to go.

31

As for drugs, they seemed too out of control for me. I was having a hard enough time trying to stay focused on what I put into my body; I couldn't bear the thought of bingeing on munchies after getting stoned. The risk was too great and counterproductive to the games I was already playing.

I didn't completely identify with the dancers who tortured their bodies on a regular basis all in the name of art. While I certainly admired their petite statures, I didn't know what it felt like to have no hips or breasts. Instead, I found and formed my own group of disenfranchised and hungry girls, and we became a club.

The Wednesday Club and 5-7-9

It started in innocence—an after-school gathering of girlfriends sharing food. Eating can be a normal and important bonding ritual in the youth culture—over French fries, allegiances are formed and deep desires revealed. I can recall giggling a lot with my friends over pizza and Coke, so much so that the carbonation threatened to fizzle up through my nose. We were five smart girls in honors and Advanced Placement classes; together we were actors, musicians, visual artists, and dancers—every discipline at our school was represented. All of us loved boys, yet only one of us, Laura, had a boyfriend. Laura was the most advanced member of our group, possessing a tight little body and a sexual résumé that seemed unreal: She'd French-kissed when she was 9, been felt up by the time she was 12, and at 16 had gotten involved in a sexual relationship with an older boy who broke her heart. Now, at 17, Laura was seeing Marcus, a gifted cellist and doting boyfriend who brought her flowers even when it wasn't a special occasion.

At 16, I rejoiced at finding what felt like normal, healthy friends. No one was threatening to beat me up or throw eggs at my house. No one called me *fat,* and better yet, no one in this group had the potential to do so either. These were sweet, sincere, and well-intentioned girls. But each one of us in our own way was very hungry—for affection, acceptance, belonging. When we got together for dinner, we spent a lot of time talking, and all of the time eating. Gossip was our main dish, but we also let some personal tidbits pass through our busy lips. It was as if our group feasts also gave us permission to purge the secrets from our lives.

Over barbecued ribs one night, Laura let it slip that her mother's boyfriend had been sexually abusing her. He crept into her room at night and fondled her while she desperately tried to pretend she was asleep . . . and he'd been doing it since she was 12. *He* was the one who'd felt her up. She brought this up to us because it was beginning to affect her ability to be intimate with Marcus. She felt like she was falling in love with him, but she couldn't accept that he really cared for her. Lately she'd even been refusing his advances, and she could tell that he was frustrated and thinking of breaking up with her. For so long, sexual activity had been associated with a dirty secret for Laura. She could replicate that behavior with other boys because it was, according to her, "no big deal," but now she felt as if she loved Marcus and wanted to tell him the truth. Needless to say, we were all stunned and ill equipped to ask the right questions, but we stumbled through it. We ate more than usual during that conversation—everyone ordered their own dessert, and our brownie sundaes helped us feel safe and secure in that difficult moment.

Laura was my ride home, and as I went to find her in the restaurant's bathroom, I could hear her vomiting. I asked if she was sick, and she said that she'd just eaten too much. It immediately hit me that she was doing what Josie did. Laura didn't say much on the ride home, but she looked more relieved and relaxed. She had just literally purged the memory of being abused and let it flush violently down the toilet. Her face revealed a sense of peace I couldn't understand. And I had no idea how she could possibly go back into that house. Yet I didn't tell anyone about Laura, and neither did the other girls. We just chalked it up to the zillions of serious and disturbing secrets we learned about our friends. Betraying that trust could make someone a social pariah.

We named our group "The Wednesday Club," and each week picked a different type of food to inhale. Although I claimed to be on a diet, I found myself indulging with the girls on Wednesdays. I was thus introduced to the notion of bingeing and the intense self-loathing that followed. I still couldn't do what Josie and Laura did—throw up after meals—but I wasn't immune to trying new things. Another girl in our group, Tina, introduced me to laxatives.

Tina was an artist who stood a few inches below the rest of us. She was stout and cute, and we all saw her rail against her stocky stature. She wanted nothing more than to be thin, so she worked out like a maniac. She first brought up laxatives over Thai food one night. "Sometimes I take 60 a day," she boasted. "I learned it from Kelly." Kelly was her best friend and a ballet dancer at our school.

"What does it do?" I asked. "Just make you poop?"

"Yes," she said. "It gets rid of everything you've eaten, and you don't have to throw up."

There was that tone in her voice that indicated that if we took laxatives instead of vomiting we'd somehow be in a more advanced category than our bulimic friends. So I decided to take laxatives for a while—sometimes 20 or 30 a day. At first they seemed to work, but then they just made me so crampy and bloated that I stopped using them. Restricting my food intake seemed to work better for me.

Probably one of the worst things we could have done following a meal was to go shopping, but try telling that to a bunch of teenage girls. We'd all take our allowances or baby-sitting money and go to the mall after dinner. This is where the women got separated from the girls. I mean, really. Tina and I were the only girls in our group who didn't fit in the "skinny" category. All of the others were wiry and lean—adding up their sizes together wouldn't even make a size 14. They shopped in a store just for them called 5-7-9. For many years that store had been off-limits to me, but one day I ventured in there, lured by the cute cutoff-jean shorts in the window. Laura admired the same pair, so we both flew in and began rifling through the rack. She found her size 5 immediately. I searched the rack hoping to find a size 12, obviously ignoring the name of the store: 5-7-9! I reluctantly grabbed the 9 off the rack and slipped into the dressing room awaiting complete and utter devastation.

I again faced a showdown with my thighs. They refused to stop rubbing against each other, even after all of these years of missed meals. I closed my eyes and began inching the jean shorts up my legs, pausing slightly at the thighs and begging them to let the seams of the shorts rise to the top. They did—and what I found at the waist was an easy snap of a button. *I fit into a size 9!* I hadn't been this small since I was in the seventh grade! I paraded out in front of the group, who had already established a support circle around Laura and her tiny legs. Mine seemed to pour out of my shorts—but I also revealed muscular calves, thanks to countless exercises I did in my room at night. I enjoyed what I saw, and for some reason didn't think it would last long, so I snatched up this pair of magical shorts and headed home to revel in my new accomplishment.

What mattered more to me was that I was able to shop in the same store as Laura and the rest of the girls—*and* I was able to wear the same short shorts. For years I'd forsaken stores like 5-7-9 because shoving my curvy body into clothes not made for me was utterly depressing. Truth is, I had no idea what size I really was. My shape had shifted so much throughout high school that I was constantly in flux. Nevertheless, I wore my shorts proudly the next day, as did Laura. By looking at us, you couldn't tell that we were wearing the same clothes, as our bodies were entirely different. But for me it was a personal triumph and a reminder that no matter how hungry I got, I wouldn't eat.

Starving Eyes and Pretend Sleeping

If there was anything I developed in high school, it was intense discipline. A master of juggling many things, I handled school, rehearsal, homework, social life, and extreme dieting like it all was a piece of forbidden cake. I settled so well into the routine of restriction that it became second nature. I never doubted or questioned the intense dislike of my being. Since I was a girl and an actress, I thought that was my lot in life. Being satisfied with my appearance was an oxymoron.

Thriving on little food and lots of obsessive thoughts, I danced around the halls in my ever-fluctuating jean sizes, barely aware of my strength and power. Being strong meant being able to not eat when others did, to withhold and prove my willpower, and to outsmart the hungry voice in my head and convince it to be satisfied on a rice cake and carrot stick. Unlike your average anorexic girl, however, I didn't have the body to match the disease. I never looked sick or remotely like Kate Moss or Tracey Gold. I didn't look like Josie. I didn't look like Laura. And I didn't look like someone who only ate 500 calories a day. What was I doing wrong? How could my body betray me like this? What else would I have to do to melt away the flesh on my thighs and belly?

It seemed that no matter how hard I tried, my body fought back and refused to budge from a size and shape that I would one day recognize as being healthy and functioning. But I didn't see it that way at 17. All I wanted to do at that time was shrink, and mold myself into what I thought I should be: an empty, pretty vessel, one who ignored her smarts, wit, and passion and instead focused on how many fat grams were in a whole-grain bagel. Yeah, that seemed right.

Soon my fellow eating-disordered friends would come to admire my dieting determination. However, in any given group of girls, I could pick out the one who wasn't eating, not by her actions but by her eyes. We shared the same dull, dying-to-eat, filled-to-the-brim-with-pain expression. It didn't matter if we had blue, green, or brown eyes—hungry eyes looked the same.

As with all semipermanent friendships in high school, I drifted in and out of the Wednesday Club. Marcus had decided that he couldn't be with Laura once he found out her dark secret. She was destroyed by this but was now very involved with a new boy named Roger, a rebounder who could keep her secret. And because he wanted to be in the army when he graduated from high school, Laura felt that Roger could protect her from her mother's boyfriend. At some point later on, Roger actually did hit this man, and for a while Laura's mom kicked her out, so she lived with Roger and his family. Soon she became so preoccupied with her own survival that she stopped going out with us.

Tina, too, had found a boyfriend, a Cuban kid named Arturo who loved her short, curvy stature. They became the couple known to French kiss anywhere at any time—they were always lip-locked and awkwardly groping. Arturo sat a good foot taller than Tina, so sometimes she'd stand on a chair to make out with him.

Coupling off became more of a priority than shoveling in our meals together. Attracting the attention of a boy's affection was second on my list of priorities after dropping weight. I was convinced that it was because I was too fat that I didn't have a boyfriend, but my love of boys and flirting brought me into the world of Sabrina and Marisol, who were new to our school. They were identical Brazilian twins who looked like they were formed from the mold of every guy's fantasy. Each stood tall, about 5'10"; and their curves began at their ample breasts and followed down to their tiny waists. Their slim hips curved in to the slope of lean, muscular legs, complete with adorable beauty marks on their knees and shins. Their hair was jet black and long, and their faces resembled exotic dolls with pin-up girls' pouts. Sabrina and Marisol exuded more sexual energy than they were even aware of, and they were quite aware of their power.

Marisol was a visual artist and a more brooding, introspective type; Sabrina was in the theater program a year behind me and was a much better flirt than actor—but each sister was a brilliant student with a mind that easily produced 1,300s on the SATs without trying. Sabrina and I bonded right away, as she was drawn to my talent and I to her beauty. Individually, we fed off of each other's insecurity and quest to be liked. And together, we made a pretty complete woman.

I loved being around Sabrina because men were drawn to her like horny magnets. We were never at a loss for a good flirt with a great-looking boy. I was well aware that they came first for Sabrina's body and then stayed for my wit. I was developing a very skewed sense of self with men, yet I longed for the relationships that my friends had. And even though Sabrina's relationships were chock-full of drama, rumors, infidelity, and jealousy, I wanted a boy to care that intensely about me. What I really wanted was that great *Afterschool Special* hero to come bounding through the door of my high school, disguised as the new kid, and fall madly in love with me over the prettier, thinner dancers and actors. I was stuck in my own twisted fairy tale.

Sabrina and Marisol had their 16th birthday party at a popular fondue restaurant, where about ten of us were to share a big pot of boiling oil, cheese, and chocolate while dipping meat, bread, and dessert items into the various pots. The thought of plunging a piece of off-limits bread into a *so* off-limits bubbling cheese crock repulsed and frightened me. My days of group bingeing with the Wednesday Club were over, for I was convinced that I'd never have a happy romantic life if I didn't lose these last 15 pounds. Consequently, I'd put myself on extra chicken duty: I cut out basically everything in my diet but baked chicken and salad makings. My body was changing drastically, and my parents took notice, but in their own distorted view of health, they saw my losing weight as an accomplishment to be praised. Since it was a goal for them, too, they congratulated my shrinkage with a shopping trip. When I could once again slip into those size-9 shorts, I knew I couldn't let go of my disappearing act—especially since I was being rewarded for not being fat. My family and friends thought I looked healthy—but we can never measure a person's true fitness body by just their body alone.

I knew I couldn't participate in the oil-dunking festivities of the night, so I carefully baked my own chicken to bring to the party. Off I went with the twins' purple-and-blue-wrapped presents under one arm and some tinfoil-wrapped chicken under the other. The strangest thing was that no one thought twice when I brought out my own baked chicken at the party, as if it wasn't unusual at all for a young girl to bring her own poultry to a restaurant. Again, I was lauded for my "discipline" and "control"—and I relished it. When everyone moaned and complained about how fattening each chocolate- or hot-oil dip was, I reveled in the fact that I was somehow better for not going giving in and being weak. Meanwhile, my chicken was so dry that I had to excuse myself and walk next door to a 7-Eleven to pick up some ketchup so I could make it through the dry bites. But I still felt like a champion.

After dinner, we all went back to the twins' house to begin a movie-and-junk-food fest that would last through the night. It didn't matter that everyone was overloaded from dinner, on the table were sundae fixings, chips, pretzels, and frozen pizzas. I watched as thin tank-topped arm after thin tank-topped arm reached for a chip, scoop of ice cream, or pretzel. Everyone in the group seemed to eat without care, without knowledge that this could make them jump up ten whole sizes by tomorrow. Or at least that's how I felt. I thought I'd get fat if I even looked at a cookie the wrong way. And if I broke with my routine now and ate junk, then I'd never stop.

The anguish over not eating or joining in on the festive night began to stress me out so much that I went into Sabrina's bedroom to lie down. And then it hit me: I could pretend I was tired—going to sleep would keep me in another room and away from the food. That way I wouldn't have to make up an excuse for why I wasn't eating the M&M's or hear people praise me for having the strength they wished they had. I didn't have strength—I was starving. And angry. But I would rather have eaten the wrapping paper on the gifts than destroy my diet. So, at the expense of bonding and laughing and spending time with friends, I pretended to be tired so that I wouldn't have to face a kitchen full of forbidden food. As I lay there with my head buried under the covers to drown out the sounds of chewing and chuckling I couldn't help but transfer this experience into a lesson of punishment: *See, you're too fat to be able to enjoy yourself like normal people.* A rush of similar negative voices went through my mind as I finally drifted off to sleep.

✳ ✳ ✳

chapter 3

Bathroom Soaps
and Snickers Bars

J osie and I shared an AP English class together, and I did both her
work and mine. It was a given that she'd sit at the desk directly
to my right and rather blatantly copy off of me whenever we had
an exam. She was shameless in her cheating, so bold in her whispers and head turns that it was almost as if she were daring our
teacher to notice. She could do the work, but that wasn't the
point. Josie was used to having things given to her.

Now 17, Josie finally seemed to have settled into the persona
of a dainty ballerina, and in that image she denied her own ability to be smart and work hard. She preferred to apply her lip gloss
than her mind. And I was her co-dependent friend, offering up my
own hard work and intelligence for her to borrow. One day, after
another round of successful school fraud, I raised my hand and
asked to go to the bathroom. I didn't really need to go, I just
needed a break.

Our bathrooms were live-action soap operas—at any given
minute you could push open the door and discover the worlds of
lying, backstabbing, cheating, romance, deception, and wicked

teenage plotting unfolding right in front of the bathroom mirror. Crumbled tissues with smeared lipstick or smudged mascara were the signs of a particularly good episode. I often got caught up in the storylines of drama involving a girl whose boyfriend cheated on her, or at least she *suspected* him of cheating, based on a note she found in his locker.

Of course I loved this stuff—I was able to escape into other people's pain, which allowed me to forget my own. Plus, I was able to see a vulnerable side to people that I didn't normally see in the guarded hallways of our school.

I also liked going to the bathroom for another reason: On the way there, I could sneak into the student lounge, where I could jam 60 cents into the machine and receive a Snickers bar in return. This was my salvation in the middle of starving season. Lying about going to the bathroom and then rushing to devour a Snickers was my own form of rebellion. Sometimes my hunger would growl so loud from my belly that I felt the only way to quell it was with a candy bar. I'd practically shove the entire thing in my mouth while moving swiftly down the hallway to the bathroom, chewing fast so that no one would catch me with the evidence. Upon entering the bathroom, I'd look for immediate traces of the Snickers revenge on my body. I checked out my butt, thighs, face, and upper arms to see if my body had betrayed me and was already announcing the fact that I'd gorged on a chocolate bar. Once I ate the Snickers, my head would be filled with thoughts of punishing exercise and hurtful dialogue that didn't allow me to rest. Yet I ate that bar— because no one expected me to, and because I was hungry.

Most days I was able to forget my sins of binge eating once I entered the tantrum-filled stalls of the rest room. I usually got sucked into the plight of Danielle, who always seemed to be worried that she was pregnant with her boyfriend, Juan's, baby. Could she give Susan Lucci a run for her money in the crying department! Usually there was an entire gaggle of supporters there to offer advice and happily miss out on class. Apparently, Danielle couldn't use birth control because her family was strictly Catholic and hadn't taught her about sex yet. Yet that didn't stop her from having sex with Juan, who I knew for a fact was also doing it with three other girls.

On this particular day, I was really looking forward to another episode of *As Danielle's World Turns* before I returned to class. Somewhat disappointed to see that no one was in the rest room, I rushed to the mirror to examine my guilty face. That's when I heard a quiet sobbing and moaning coming from the last stall. I stopped chewing and listened to the pain spilling out from behind door number three. I couldn't tell who belonged to those cries, but I *did* know that something terrible had happened.

I asked through the slate-gray door if the person was okay. No answer. "Do you need me to get somebody?" I ventured. No answer. I tried again: "Are you sure you're okay?" even though it was obvious that this person wasn't. The sound I heard went beyond crying—it was a soul breaking, a deep anguish being let out in small tiny whimpers and a barely audible whisper.

"*No, no, no, no, no . . . ,*" she said over and over again, as if the words were rocking her to sleep. I felt compelled to stay, yet I was a little scared to see who was behind the crying. Finally, I heard the latch unlock and the stall door slowly opened. Maya Gibbons shuffled out looking like a zombie, her face puffy from many hours of crying.

Maya was a theater major in my grade. She was a sweet African-American girl with tight curly hair and gigantic warm eyes who came from a poor neighborhood in Miami and who had worked very hard to get into this school. I was made aware of her personal economic struggle when we did a scene together in acting class and she confided in me that she what she wanted most was to be able to wear designer duds just like her best friends, Vanessa and Rhonda. Maya felt embarrassed that her mother could barely afford to keep her in new clothes let alone ones with trendy brand names.

Yet Maya's desire to have better clothes didn't consume her like it did others—she was always smiling and often greeted people with a hug. What we all loved most about her was her laugh, which seemed to pop out of her nose in a half snort that made us laugh even harder when we heard it. She always seemed to be laughing, and while she wasn't the most competitive actor in class, Maya seemed happy to be where she was and who she was. She had a real sense of confidence that I admired.

Once Maya saw that I was the only one in the bathroom, she let out a big wail that zapped me into mother/nurturer mode, and I started pulling tissues out from the holder on the wall and wiping her tears. We eventually embraced, and her body felt limp and lifeless. When she spoke, she barely made a sound, and although she could hug me, she couldn't look me in the eyes as she told me what had happened.

Maya had seen, heard, and smelled death—all in her own house the previous night. While she and her brothers were doing homework and watching TV, their mother's boyfriend murdered their mother in the bedroom. He chopped her up with an ax, systematically cutting off her arms and legs. Maya had heard moans and muffled yells coming from her mother's room, but she and her siblings had been warned not to disturb her mother and her boyfriend when they were in the bedroom because that usually meant they were being romantic. Her younger brother had once caught his mother and her boyfriend in the act and had been punished for it, so no matter what they heard going on, the kids didn't interfere. Maya and the boys had also heard some fighting, but that wasn't a surprise either, since the boyfriend beat their mother and had also hit Maya. Unfortunately, as events in the bedroom turned grisly, Maya and her brothers tried to drown out their mother's sounds by turning up the volume of the TV. The boyfriend was able to slip out their mother's window, and she hadn't even been discovered until that morning. Missing the bus to school, Maya had gone to her mother's room to ask for a ride and had found the remains of her mother in her bed.

To bear witness to one's childhood vanishing is a horrible sight. I was well aware that Maya might recover from this in future years, but her life had been irrevocably altered and her innocence forever shattered. The magnitude wasn't lost on me, but appropriate action was. I felt like vomiting. I cried with her, but I was mostly silent and in awe of her strength in coming to school. Apparently she didn't have much extended family, so the relatives that were called to the scene that morning urged the children to go to school in an attempt to get back to "normal."

The thought that somehow school could house a space for Maya to feel safe after what she'd witnessed disgusted me. No wonder she sought refuge in the bathroom stall. She was in shock. So was I. The bathroom soap opera had taken a devastating, gruesome turn.

The first time you intimately experience death as a child is life altering. All at once, your safe world is violated and shifted, and a greater grown-up sense is unfairly installed, causing you to absorb and ponder things differently. As Maya told me her story, I immediately flashed back to my first experience with death. It was also a shocking murder, but of a sweet friend, not a family member.

Billy and I had fallen in puppy love at a summer retreat for my dad's company that magically took place at Disney World. Billy's stepmother was an executive along with my father, and his father was poised to become the next attorney general of Florida. Billy was raised in elite private schools and was loaded with preppie good looks and charm. He was the closest I'd ever come to seeing my *Afterschool Special* hero realized: He was older (16), adorable, and saw something special in me, even though I was only 13. Although our relationship never progressed to deep romance, it elicited those delicious and necessary beautiful memories that one could live off for years. When Billy and I were together, we knew that somewhere in an alternate universe, our souls had conspired this friendship.

Months after that summer, I was preparing for my bat mitzvah. Billy was set to sit at my table even though those spots are traditionally reserved for family. Every night before I drifted off to sleep, I imagined my reunion with Billy—I couldn't wait to make him laugh and tell our inside jokes again. One morning at about six, my mother sat on my bed whispering through my sleepiness and begging me to get up. I didn't need to get up for another hour, yet there was something "off" in the sound of my mother's voice. I opened my eyes rather abruptly to find my father silently standing behind her with his head down. Even though these signs were new to me, my gut was telling me that something was wrong.

My parents ushered me into their bedroom, where they then sat down on both sides of me and held my hands. I still didn't know enough to freak out, so I just listened. My mother began: "Listen, you know how sick Billy's mom is, right? Well, last night, there was an accident. Billy's mother is dead."

Mom wasn't talking about his stepmother or else she would have used her name, Madeline. Instead, she meant Billy's biological mother, who I knew had some serious emotional issues and was forced to live apart from Billy all last year. My mind immediately conjured up a situation where Billy now had to live with us for a while. (I completely ignored the lack of logic in this imagined scenario, but it's funny that this is where my mind went.)

My mother then continued, destroying my fantasy. "Billy's mother killed herself last night," she choked through tears, "and she . . . killed . . . Billy, too."

My head dropped into the pillow and swirling, silent emotions ripped through my body, even though I was unaware of my existence at that moment. Everything became empty with blended time and space. I knew I was crying because I could taste the salt on my lips, but I didn't feel sadness, anger, or *anything*. I was truly in shock. Up until this point, I hadn't known death—not of a grandparent or relative or neighbor. And I certainly didn't know *violent* death.

As if someone had released the mute button, my noisy grief came into full volume, and I let out wails and cries that I didn't realize my body could house. I started to hyperventilate, and my howls awoke my sister, Becky, who had no idea that my world had just lost its sugary coating. My parents explained to me as best they could in between their own anguished crying that Billy's mother had picked him up after school and had driven him into a dilapidated section of downtown Miami, saying she needed to get the car repaired. She then got out of the car, walked to Billy's side, pulled out a gun, and shot her only son—her own flesh and blood—at least four times at close range. She then went to a phone booth, dialed 911, told them what had happened, and put a bullet in her own head.

"Why?!" I echoed many times that morning, as if someone would have a logical reason for such an act.

My father tried his best to explain the motive: "Billy's mom was very sick, Jessie. She feared losing full custody of Billy when his dad won the election." The previous night, Billy's father had indeed been elected as our state's attorney general.

I somehow got dressed that morning in between following the news reports on TV and the morning radio programs. Billy's murder was high profile, yet they were missing the point. This wasn't just a politician's son who was killed—this was the sweetest soul on Earth, a loving jokester, a potential boyfriend, and a good boy who had every reason to believe that he'd grow up to be an even better man.

The death of Billy rattled my naïveté and challenged my faith in God. For a brief time it took me completely away from my inner turmoil and body loathing and transported me into a space where I recognized that others felt this kind of pain all the time. Every single day someone somebody loves dies, and that kind of greater human awareness settled into my sensitive soul.

I hadn't thought about Billy for quite a while. I'd buried him somewhere, along with all of those cozy memories and a good dose of denial. Or was it transition and moving on? Either way, the experience became a sleeve on the coat of my adolescent discoveries. As I held Maya years later, I realized how blessed I was to have a family that loved me and to live in a house where I felt safe—two things Maya would never feel again. I felt ashamed and astonished that minutes before I'd spoken to this wounded girl, the biggest concern I'd had was my Snickers-binge routine and how it might affect my waistline. This dose of reality was more than I could handle. My world was once again busted wide open, and I was forced to consider a much larger playing field. I ached and grieved for Maya. I shed some more of my innocence that day, and the seeds of greater emotional and social responsibility were deeply planted within my heart.

For months I couldn't shake the story that Maya had shared with me that day. I wondered how many other people had secrets like Laura or Josie, or felt the intense pain that Maya had. I was slowly being awakened to a more complex and grown-up world.

The ability to absorb eating disorders, sexual abuse, and murder into the fiber of my high school experience only helped to chip away at my myopic existence. In our youth, we're so resilient and willing to hold great space for many dramatic lessons, not knowing fully how each interaction will play out in the long-term development of our identity.

The remainder of my high school days moved forward with equal parts pain and joy. Everyone—including Maya—managed to make it through graduation and focus on what we thought would surely be the answer to our quest for a happiness, social relief, and autonomy: life after high school.

Things returned to a familiar climate, and I continued to wrestle with my hungry identity that now had in its supply of emotions some colorful, rich, and deep experiences. I was still an empty vessel, but there was the promise of becoming full.

✳ ✳ ✳

chapter 4

24-Hour Pizza and More Secrets

The space between high school and college holds a million possibilities. My mind was flush with fantasies of what my roommate and I would do on Friday nights, what kinds of all-nighters I'd pull, and what sort of zesty flirtations I'd have with older, wiser boys. Flashes of my independence and new identity melded together to create a composite of images from liquor, clothing, and MTV ads. But that's what's so magical about college—it's a fresh period of time when you enter into a world of assumed grown-up responsibilities coupled with the lingering desire to remain adolescent and immature.

I thought that all of my problems would vanish in college. I'd meet amazing people, do well academically, fall madly in love, and figure out who and what I wanted to be . . . all before graduation. Most of that *did* happen—but not as I'd originally imagined.

If you're a young woman between the ages of 13 and 18, then I'm sure you've heard what happens to you when you get to

college. In addition to the not-so-urban legends involving screaming freedom, raucous keg parties, and intense romance, you're
regaled with tales of the infamous "Freshmen 15." These mythic stories of hot young bodies turning into flabby, pizza-encrusted couch
potatoes all within the first semester seemed to haunt me in particular. So, as much as I wanted to believe that I could leave behind
my disdain for my curves, I carried my tradition of body hatred
straight into college. Spending the entire summer before working
out and severely dieting, I managed to not only develop a great tan
and sharp calf muscles, but a hunger that stretched even deeper into
my soul. Hunger and excitement for who I was to meet. Hunger and
fear that I had no idea what the next four years would hold. Hunger
and desire to shed my former self and feel good in my skin.

I chose to attend Penn State University, a huge, gorgeous school
that's smack-dab in the middle of Pennsylvania. The area boasts
green mountains and a rainy season that ranks third in the nation.
The concept of bundling up for the winter was lost on this Florida
girl, so when my mother and I went shopping for my first winter
coat, I managed to ask this question from under the face flap of my
down jacket: "How do people at this school hook up?" For me, the
idea of attracting the opposite sex involved showing at the very least
a tan tummy or toned arms that shot out of a form-fitting tank top.
Growing up in a state where people don't have to (much less want
to) wear a lot of clothing gave me a skewed perception of court-
ing, flirting, and dating. It really was ironic that after all this time
I'd spent starving and sweating away my body, now I was just
going to cover it up with long johns, a sweater, and a jacket.

I picked Penn State for its theater program and academic
opportunities—I kind of just ignored the weather component.
Besides, when I visited the campus, it fulfilled every one of those
Afterschool Special scenarios: football teams, cheerleaders, and a
"normal" atmosphere that I wouldn't find at the arts schools in
downtown Miami. I thought Penn State would be the perfect place
to finally blend in and become like everyone else. I was so wrong.

By the fourth week of school, I was without a roommate. I
started with a girl named Candy, who went home after two weeks

because her boyfriend lured her back to attend their local community college. My pre-college fantasy of finding a new best friend in my roommate and forming a relationship where we did everything together was quickly shattered. Yet, even during those two weeks, Candy and I had barely spoken. She thought my "theater thing" was weird, and the only time we ever had a real conversation was during one of the first nights in our dorm room, when we shared a pizza at 1:00 A.M.

In college, normal dining hours take on a definition of their own, as you have a slew of places at your disposal that are ready to deliver such nutritious treats as pizzas, hoagies, wings, and sodas to your door at all hours of the night. In fact, it's sort of a college tradition to have the pizza-delivery person come to your room during those hours when most people are in a deep slumber. So Candy and I took part in the rite. Never mind that I hadn't eaten pizza in two years. I ate that night in the hopes of bonding, and creating remarkable memories with my new roommate. Instead, I was filled with regret, guilt, and body anxiety. I tried to explain some of this to Candy, and she said, "I just don't get girls who throw up their food. That is, like, so gross and totally sick."

Clearly, Candy and I weren't going to see eye-to-eye on this one, so my eating disorder remained tucked away inside my mind. After Candy's exit, I thought that I'd be assigned a new roommate—*now* I'd meet my new best friend. But no one was ever assigned to me. To some, this would have been a great coup and a coveted position; to me, it was a lonely way to spend my first year—and there was too much space for me to be alone with my destructive thoughts.

I wish I could have explained to Candy that eating disorders afflict the most intelligent, intense, emotionally sensitive and over-achieving beings on the planet. We're people pleasers, control freaks, girls on the verge of greatness, and ambitious to our core. Today, I'm amazed by how much I was able to pull off in the outside world while I was a total wreck on the inside. I had a sense of bravado that led me to appear to be a confident person, yet I worried constantly about my weight that first semester, which was really my lasting attempt at controlling a new environment. And what made it so much easier to stay hidden in the world of eating disorders was the fact that my entire (female) residence hall seemed to be obsessed with their weight, too. Each and every one of us wanted to avoid the Freshmen 15 at all costs. Fat was so clearly our enemy, yet we embraced it nightly on our late-night pizza binges.

As we rallied against our changing bodies and rigorous schedules, some of us fared better than others. For example, Amy lived down the hall and always seemed to be at the top of her game. She worked out daily, barely ate anything destructive, got good grades, and even had a boyfriend. I watched her in envy because I couldn't even figure out how to wake up in time for class. Yet the illusion of Amy came crashing down when I heard her vomiting in the bathroom in the middle of the afternoon.

I'd come home to change for a dance class one day, and the silence of the hall was broken by the sounds of violent retching coming from the bathroom. Fearing that one of the girls was really sick, I went in to see what was up. From under the stall I could make out Amy's long blonde ponytail and slim white ankle folded underneath her leg. She was crying as well as throwing up, so I asked her if I should get our resident advisor (R.A.) or call the school infirmary.

"No!" she screamed.

"Okay," I said, backing off.

As I was ready to exit the bathroom, she confessed, "I'm just having a hard time getting it to come up today, and it's stinging my throat. I ran out of ipecac, so I used a plastic spoon and it just hurts." She spoke so matter-of-factly, as if I knew her bulimic routine and could understand her frustration.

I wondered why she was telling me this *and* why I kept coming in contact with bathroom confessions from women in deep emotional pain. I felt as if I was cursed to be the one let in on everyone's dark secrets. I had one of my own, you know—no one would have guessed looking at me that I, too, was struggling. After all, my demons wrestled internally instead of winding up in the toilet bowl at odd hours of the day.

I was frozen in place—I didn't want to leave Amy alone, yet I was desperate to get away from this situation. She flushed the toilet and came out of the stall, rinsed her mouth out, and splashed some water on her face. She turned to me, ponytail swinging defiantly, and said, "How else do you think I manage to keep it together?"

She blew by me and left me there alone with those words dancing in my head. Her comment was such a blatant reference to her image. She knew that we thought she had it all together and this comment was equal parts sarcasm, anger, and rebellion. Again I held on to another girl's secret, and from that moment on, I declined joining in on the gossip regarding her seeming perfection. I'd seen the truth.

The weirdest piece of this puzzle came from a poster in the very bathroom where Amy and I'm sure countless others purged their daily issues. It read: EATING DISORDERS CAN KILL. And written underneath it in black marker was: FUCK YOU, I'M ALREADY DEAD.

An Ingénue and Mark

As new theater majors, we were warned that freshmen *never* got cast in main stage productions. Our department boasted not only a healthy undergrad program but also a nationally recognized graduate school, so competing for parts was intense. There simply wasn't enough material to keep everyone working. And in some way, our faculty thought that it was a perfect metaphor for what "real life" would hold for us after college. "Acting is a competitive business and you should expect to fail" was a mantra repeated by many intense professors who were all still nursing their own "real-life" wounds.

There's a side of me that I've always liked and until now didn't fully recognize, and that's my sheer determination to succeed. Hearing the word *no* just spurred me on to work harder. I was probably helped along by my serious performing-arts school training and oppressive leadership from Roy Avery and countless others. I thrived as the underdog. So when it was time for my first college audition, I prepared with a fury. My discipline paid off, for I was the only freshman cast in both main shows my first semester. I was ecstatic. Finally, I was going to rewrite my personal history and insert a new finale chock-full of achievement and acceptance. I was 18 and was expected to play opposite 30-year-old grad students, so naturally I was the ingénue. The directors who cast me saw me as a leading lady, a love interest, a temptress—images that I'd erased from my mind years ago and replaced with a grotesque non-sexual image of a fat character actor. I guess these professors didn't get the memo sent from my earlier teachers that I wasn't pretty enough to be a leading lady.

No one knew what I looked like before college. It was as if my body held on tightly to our secret as it released the weight and held me steady at a size 9. Ironically, I never felt the jubilation of reaching my goal in weight loss. I was always too busy obsessing about how easily it could be taken away from me. How with one slip, it could all be over. . . .

I remember walking home after seeing for myself that my name appeared on the top of that first cast list. I didn't know what to do with the rush of emotion coming from within. Everything I was doing to myself and believing about myself was being challenged. Could they, those murderous teachers of low self-esteem, have been wrong? Or was this some cruel joke or jaded dream I'd awaken from with a scream? Again, I kept this internal banter to myself and began preparing for the roles no one was supposed to get as a freshman. This fact wasn't lost on my fellow acting students—I instantly became separated from the group and felt their angst and jealousy. However, I was flourishing in the department and working nonstop. In addition to the two main stage roles, I was asked to be in a student production of a show entitled *Not Just Fooling Around,* which dealt with sexual relationships, sexually transmitted diseases, and sexual morality. *Me?* A girl who had barely had her first kiss by the time she graduated high school and was clearly the last remaining virgin on campus? It was too funny.

I was riding high from my theatrical achievements, and my exuberance showed in my step. At the very same time, I was flirting with a boy named Mark who lived in a nearby fraternity house. He looked like a leading man, with blond wavy locks, clear gray-blue eyes, and a perfectly formed grin that made my tummy turn inside out. And he was even in a fraternity, which was another notch on my pre-college fantasy belt. But best of all, *he liked me!*

The actual time line of dating in college is seriously condensed: You can fall in love in one night, and weeks can seem like months. After dating Mark for three weeks, everything seemed to be going according to plan. I mean, how much more normal could I get—I had a good-looking guy, a thriving theater career, classes that (so far) were manageable, and, oh yeah, self-esteem that seemed to be making a comeback. It would seem that I couldn't be happier.

Mark knew I was a virgin. And try as he might, I wouldn't sleep with him. By the fourth week, the sexual game of let's-see-how-much-pressure-we-can-put-on-Jessica was growing tired. Where had my hero gone? Instead, I found myself with a horny frat boy who seemed to like my body much more than my mind. I was complaining about this a couple of weeks later to Jonathon, my costar in *Not Just Fooling Around,* after rehearsing a scene where our characters go about negotiating their sexual relationship perfectly. In the play, Jonathon embodied the ideal partner who listens to his girlfriend and agrees not to have sex before either one is ready. "Do men like this really exist?" I asked him.

"Of course they do—I'm one of them," he brazenly answered back, full-on flirting but still humble. Suddenly I was smitten with this sweet man who was going to rescue me from Prince Charming.

Rehearsals became a way for Jonathon and me to spend as much time together as possible. His unassuming nature reached out and embraced me in safety and comfort. We talked about so many things, and I could tell by looking at him that he loved me. We made sure that no physical lines were crossed when we were together, but it was becoming more and more difficult. I knew I had to do something. While Mark was my original version of college romance, Jonathon was turning out to be something more magical, and I wanted to pursue this relationship. I didn't want to hurt anyone, yet I didn't want to let this feeling go. Was I starring in my own soap opera or what? But I was determined not to make the same mistakes I'd seen my favorite characters make—there would be no lying! I'd be honest and forthright.

I made plans to come clean to Mark. For the first time in a long time, I wasn't thinking about my weight or body size—I was living in the present, enjoying my life, and feeling good about myself. I was so clearly in love, and Mark must have seen that, too.

When I showed up at his frat house, he was drinking a beer and watching a football game. I realized that I had no idea how to start—after all, I'd never broken up with anyone before. I so dearly didn't want to hurt Mark that I fumbled with my words for a while until they finally poured out: "I think I've met someone else who I'm falling in love with and I wanted to be fair and tell you now so that I didn't hurt you."

Mark stared at me, then smiled and said, "It's okay, Jess. That's totally cool. I still want to be friends. Let's just hang out and drink a beer, all right?"

I was elated that he understood and relieved to have done the right thing. I drank a beer, and Mark downed what must have been his fifth or sixth. I knew he was drunk because his voice grew louder, he started screaming orders at the quarterback on TV, his gray-blue eyes grew hazy, and the "charm" in Prince Charming drained away with each gulp of beer.

It was when Mark was this drunk that he'd usually pressure me for sex. I'd manage to maneuver around each invitation until he'd pass out. The next morning, he'd barely be able to recall his behavior, so I'd let it go. Now, in the middle of the afternoon, he was toasted and hitting on me once again. He leaned over to kiss me, and I recoiled. "What are you doing?" I screeched. "I just told you I liked someone else! I only want to be friends."

Mark scooted closer. "I know, it's just that you're so sexy to me," he slurred. "Let me just kiss you one last time."

My ego soaked up any reference at all to my sex appeal, and I was so intent on not hurting Mark's feelings that I ignored my own. I gave him one soft kiss, thinking that it would end my responsibility to him and that Jonathon would never know I had been unfaithful to our new connection. But Mark didn't want to stop at one kiss. He kept putting his lips on my neck, my arm, and my hands, until I pushed him away. He apologized over and over again, saying that he was trying to hide how much I'd hurt him and how much he was going to miss me.

The fact that this attractive male wanted me so badly was like fuel to my damaged self-esteem and warped any clear thinking in the moment. But luckily, my sixth sense kicked in and I got up and moved toward the door. Mark came up from behind me, closed the door with his hand, and kept it closed by pressing on it. The door was without a doorknob but rather had a handle and dead bolt. I tried to pry his fingers off of the door so that I could leave. My body was pumping with adrenaline—I wasn't sure what was going on, but this was a side of Mark I'd never seen before.

I turned around to face him, only to catch his knuckles on my cheek as he coldcocked me across the face. I crumbled to the floor with shock, and a pain I'd never felt before. Up until this point, I'd never been hit by anyone, other than a spanking on the rear end by one of my parents. I couldn't have imagined the pain of a human fist against my face or the stark knowledge that he planned on doing it again and perhaps would do even worse things to me.

I collapsed onto a heap of tools Mark was using to construct a loft in his room, my body merging with the cold tools and white instructions on the floor. This is how I know there's a God. Although this part is a little blurry, I do remember realizing that Mark had one hand on the door as the other hand was grabbing my hair. I reached for an object, any object, and my fingers found the blunt end of a screwdriver, which I raised straight up in the air and into Mark's groin. He howled, let go of my hair and the door, and fell to the ground wailing. I got up and ran down the hall of his fraternity house. I didn't even notice that one of the sheets of paper had been stuck to my calf. And I don't think I made a sound—I just ran and ran.

The tender pink welt on my cheek couldn't hold a candle to the searing sting of guilt and shame I was feeling inside. I didn't say a word about what had happened with Mark to anyone. I didn't think I had a right to be upset. I thought it was my fault, that I'd somehow forced him to hit me and treat me like a piece of trash. I entered into the stereotypical world of self-blame that I'd read about in pamphlets. I blamed myself for everything—for being there in his room, for drinking, for not getting up and leaving right away, for kissing him, and for letting him kiss me. I didn't wonder why he'd turned violent, or see his hitting me or coming on to me after I stated a clear boundary as a violation of my rights. I never questioned his drunken begging for sex as a blatant disregard for my personal safety. I didn't think something like this could happen to me. And then I thought I may have been overreacting—after all, I hadn't been raped. I got away, *and* I impaled him as I left, so I was lucky, wasn't I? I'd heard worse stories, so I felt as if I didn't really have anything to complain about. And the next day, there was no evidence of what Mark had done to me.

I kept the details of this painful night from Jonathon, but it showed up again in fragments and snippets of memory on the night that we made love for the first time. While it was mutual, tender, loving, and everything you would hope for in a first intimate encounter, I couldn't ignore the gnawing shame of that night with Mark. I had a sharp pain that ached inside me—but on the night of my first sexual experience, I chose to bury it along with my personal lambasting. Instead, I threw myself into the gentleness of Jonathon.

Fooling Around in The HUB

In the main stage shows during my freshman year, I embodied a Greek war refugee in *Trojan Women* and a courtesan and troll in *Peer Gynt,* but it was my performance in *Not Just Fooling Around* that forever shifted how I felt as an actor. The subject matter was close to home and relevant to the lives of the audience who came to see us in The HUB, the central student center on campus. And it was certainly relevant in my life, as I'd just experienced that horrible incident with Mark. *Not Just Fooling Around* dealt with couples in varying stages of communication issues. My scenes with Jonathon involved young lovers deciding when it was right to have sex. We giggled at the significant parallels in our lives.

One scene dealt with a homosexual couple and the choice to come out to parents and friends; another had to do with a total player who discovers that he's contracted an STD; and one scene involved a young woman who feels that she was assaulted by a date. Our student director had the idea that we should all stay in character following the production and entertain questions from the audience, essentially improvising the answers while remaining faithful to our character's background and motivation. It sounded fun in theory, and I loved to improvise, so I thought nothing of it.

After our first performance ended, we took questions from the audience. Each person who wanted to speak to us in character had to line up behind a microphone in the auditorium so as to be heard by the crowd of about 200. At first most questions had to do with the homosexual couple and whether or not they thought homosexuality was a sin. I had to remind myself that we went to school in central Pennsylvania and the student body tended to be conservative. I watched as the actors portraying these characters did brilliant work maneuvering between their character's thoughts and the responsibility we had as actor/educators.

None of us, however, was prepared for what happened next. A young woman approached the mike and said, "I relate to the girl who thinks she was raped by her date because the same thing happened to me."

I immediately thought about what had just happened with Mark and how many other women sitting out there might have experienced the same thing. A silence fell over the audience, and those who were turned off by prior questions were now taking notice. "Go on, what happened to you?" the actress who played this role prompted.

"Well, he seemed to be a great guy, and all night he behaved himself—until he got so drunk that he just pushed and pulled at me until I finally gave in and gave him what he wanted."

The crowd groaned in response. Some weren't sure that she could call that rape or assault or even forced sex because she'd used the words "gave him."

But before a debate could ensue, another voice chimed in. "The same thing happened to me," said a girl in overalls who stood at the microphone at the other side of the hall.

"And to my roommate," another voice added, this time from the front of the crowd.

No one said much after that, for the voices had spoken for themselves. This was something that until now I'd only seen at the climactic end of Lifetime movies. But these women weren't actors, and their lines hadn't been written for them.

While we were packing up our props from the show, a line of students who wanted to continue the dialogue formed at the front of the stage. This time they wanted to speak to us out of character—they wanted to know what it was like for us to do this kind of work and make such a difference. It hadn't dawned on me that we were doing that. The fact that a play, something we'd performed, helped people to find the strength to be real amazed me and made me so proud to be a part of it. I felt as if I'd done more than recite someone else's lines—I'd acted my way into their hearts by speaking their words and telling their stories. It added a depth to my interest in performing and carved out a hunger for more creative audience interaction. That night, I felt that I was a part of something greater than myself.

The rest of my freshmen year zoomed by at a breakneck pace, and I found a respite from my activity by meeting Jonathon every day at The HUB for a giant chocolate-chip cookie. Our snack break became our time to kiss, cuddle, and fall more deeply in love. I ate more when I was with Jonathon, as I pretended to be a girl with no baggage, no body-image issues, and no hurtful experiences with men. I escaped into my new relationship and I let it define me . . . for as long as I could.

The more I moved away from acknowledging what had happened with Mark, the softer I became, disappearing behind chubby mouthfuls of food and alcohol. Soon marijuana became another tool I could use to feel numb, tune out, and forget what I was feeling. I discovered that Jonathon was a regular user—he actually smoked numerous times throughout the day, and as time went by, it seemed that he couldn't do anything without being high anymore. At first I resisted joining in with him, afraid of feeling out of control and permanently messing up my image of "the good girl." Yet that out-of-control feeling called to me, as I realized it gave me permission to say things I wouldn't say and eat things I'd never allow myself to eat when I was high. Because everyone experiences the munchies when stoned, I found a great outlet for bingeing.

When my thoughts or emotions caught up with me during the day, I'd find myself looking forward to getting high so that I could zone out and forget. Jonathon proudly partook of the hippie lifestyle, complete with growing his own pot and wearing hemp clothing. Three years later, Jonathon's lifestyle would wind up being big news on campus when he got busted for dealing drugs to an undercover police officer.

By that time, I was gone and in love again.

✳ ✳ ✳

chapter 5

Finding My Voice

"You can either be a rah-rah girlfriend or an actor!"

This came from the head of the theater department at the end of my freshman year. My greatest champion was expressing how disappointed she'd become in my lapsing list of priorities. Where I'd started the year fighting ferociously for every part, I ended the year barely making call times and even arriving to rehearsals hungover and high.

I was mortified and didn't need another signal to tell me something had to change. My relationship with Jonathon had slowed to a crawl, with both of us knowing that the end was near. I'd accomplished so much during my first year of school, yet I felt as if I had nothing to show for it except poor decisions and lots of regret.

Creatively I was tapped out, having long forgetting the incredible feeling of connection and inspiration I'd felt after my performance of *Not Just Fooling Around*. Now I wasn't inspired—I was scared. I looked back at my freshman year and realized that I'd spent almost the entire time with Jonathon and his buddies and didn't have any connections or friends for myself. Not recognizing who I was and not sure who I wanted to become, I enrolled in summer school and decided to sublet an apartment on my own.

Jonathon helped me move, and before he unloaded the last box, we broke up. It was excruciating, but it was mutual. The rush of falling in love and being saved had worn off, and a new flavor of reality was here. I couldn't deny my misery, and I couldn't escape the nagging fear that I had no idea who I really was. I closed the door to my new apartment, lay down on the maroon carpet, and cried. I felt as if at any moment the earth would split from the sounds of my pain and just swallow me up. Or at least I wished it would.

Angry Women and the Female Form

"That class is for angry women," the clerk said as he rang me up at the student bookstore. "I've seen a lot of the women who take that class, and they look so damn mean, like they're about to kill some men." Clearly this guy wasn't the poster child for Women's Studies 100. I didn't know what to expect by taking this class, but I knew what I was hoping for. I wanted to figure out just what the heck had gone on with me last year—where did my identity, my voice, and my vision go? What if I was supposed to be filling myself up with the pure juices of life, and instead I'd filled up with cheap beer?

There was definitely a certain stigma associated with taking women's studies, as that politically incorrect bookseller had pointed out. You were viewed as a man-hating lesbian, a radical activist, or a "feminazi." I wasn't any of the above, although, at the time, any identity other than my own seemed appealing.

I was shocked to discover men in my class: an older gentleman who was returning to school for his sociology degree and a young cute frat boy. I entertained the thought that perhaps it was under a pledging dare that this guy took a women's-studies course during summer school, but I soon dismissed that notion as being too cruel for even a fraternity hazing. Two other men joined our class on the second day—and from the Depeche Mode stickers and pink triangles pinned on their book bags, I astutely deduced that they were gay.

The rest of the class was held together by a smorgasbord of women of all shapes, sizes, and colors. I instantly felt at home, even though I didn't really match, or fit into, any group. It had always seemed to be like that for me, but this time I had a sense of ease with my existence and somehow knew I was getting ready to go on a journey. What I loved most about this class was that I was given permission to speak about things relating to being a woman without having to apologize for it. We looked at political, social, and educational issues from all sides but spent most of the time learning about these events from a woman's perspective. This meant that I learned about female pioneers and trendsetters who were left out of the male canon of literature and history in my other classes.

It was when we spoke of current topics affecting women that I truly began to come back to life. The discussions on rape and sexual abuse grew intense and heated in our class. Some women felt safe and shared their personal stories; others resisted because men were present and they still held on to shame about their bodies and what had been done to them. The class sometimes held the atmosphere of a group-counseling session, mostly because our teacher allowed anything and everything to be discussed. It was her thought that in order for true healing to take place within women, we had to have the pendulum swing back into balance. She recognized that many women in class were angry, as the stereotypes alluded, but they weren't only angry at men. They were angry with parents, social pressure, laws, cultural values, religion, school, peers; and angry that injustice, oppression, and hatred existed in women's lives all over the world. It was a long-overdue anger, a justified anger, and an anger that when fully expressed would yield to healing.

When we got to the topic of body image, I paid particular attention, for I'd never heard a formal discussion on this issue. We looked at the female form as it was portrayed via art and photography throughout the ages. We examined the female body as a political tool, a social statement, a life-bearing gift, and an expression of soul. We explored the media images we consumed, created, and paid for with our hard-earned money. We examined our cultural beliefs related to being a woman and the value our society placed on appearance and youthfulness.

We learned about power and food, fat and rage, identity and strength. As my mind and worlds were expanding through this class, I found that I ate more and more to suppress all of the feelings and ideas I was having. I grew achingly uncomfortable in my skin, and applying layers of new information from this class made me feel as if I would burst.

One night I found myself in front of my toilet contemplating vomiting—I really wanted to just throw up the past year of my life. I thought about Laura and Josie and Amy and all of the other women I knew who did this every day and seemed to be just fine, even though I knew they weren't. I thought about how I might do this tonight and never stop.

As I contemplated purging my dinner, I had an epiphany, yet another sign for me that there was a God. I felt a presence and heard a voice that told me if I took the step to begin purging my food that night I would die. It wasn't a manly "Godlike" voice coming down from a mountaintop, but rather a soft, sweet, feminine voice. My intuition, inner guides, and angels came through to tell me that at this fork in the road, I could choose death or rebirth. So many times death had seemed like a great choice for me, but in this moment I chose life. In that one instant, I visualized a new life, one where I would become me—fully.

Before class the next day, I took my teacher aside and said, "Listen, a lot of what we're talking about in here is really affecting me, especially the parts about body image. I think I need to get some help." I couldn't believe I was admitting this, but as the words poured out of my mouth, I knew I was doing the right thing. She suggested that I visit the counseling center, and I went there immediately after class.

The counselor on duty was a kind woman named Melissa who wore gigantic round glasses and also served as the nutritionist. *Perfect*, I thought. *My issue is with food and how it controls me, so she can finally tell me what I'm supposed to eat.* So my voices may have gotten me to counseling, but they obviously hadn't enlightened me completely.

I believed that food was the enemy, and the culprit behind my barely there self-esteem. I told Melissa that what I needed was a consistent food plan to follow so that I could feel more in control. She said that we'd talk about food eventually, but first she wanted to find out about my family. *Why?* I wondered. *Clearly it's my lack of control with food that got me here—my family's fine, great, let's talk about food!*

Melissa began to ask me about my parents and their views of their bodies when the truth suddenly came tumbling out of my mouth. I told her all about my family's longtime history of struggling with their weight.

She listened and replied, "I think you should join our eating-disorders group. It meets every week, and I think you'll get a lot out of it."

That didn't sound right to me. Amy, Laura, and Josie had eating disorders. They threw up; I didn't. I wasn't super-skinny and didn't look sick. I merely dabbled in dieting and exercise—I didn't have a full-blown eating disorder. I didn't connect the dots that what I was feeling and experiencing were the very signs of someone who's struggling. So I joined the group, and every Thursday for the next four years I entered into a space where lives were changed forever.

Summer Love and the Circles of Silence

In the midst of the great personal transformation I was going through, I was also falling in love again.

Along with my women's studies class, I was also taking a speech communication course. (That summer I took eight credits, and not a one really applied to my major—but they all applied to the development of *me*.) Our first assignment was to interview another person in class and then get up and deliver an oral presentation about what we'd discovered about them. *Piece of cake!* I thought. I searched the room to see who on first glance showed promise as a juicy interview subject.

As I auditioned people with my eyes, the class's resident cynic, Ken, interrupted me. "I guess I'll do you," he said with apathy, as if I'd been the very last choice for him.

"Gee, thanks," I said, "but I wanted to interview . . . " I trailed off, noticing that in the time it took to try to worm my way out of being with Ken, the class had paired off, and I was stuck with him. Asking questions about his upbringing was a marvelous lesson in patience: He loved to talk about himself but rarely made sense, as if he was trying on other people's sentences. As he rambled, I struggled to find a few gems that I could use in class the next day. On the other hand, I thought that I'd given Ken the interview of his life. I spoke of politics and social values and thought I sounded quite eloquent. But what came out of Ken's mouth during his presentation really pissed me off: "So, yeah, Jessica just broke up with her boyfriend and is real lonely this summer, so she decided to take a women's studies class to bond with some other chicks."

What? First of all, those statements were made off the record and not in that sequence at all. What I'd shared with Ken as small talk after our interview is what he chose to present to the class. Either my brilliance was lost on Ken or he truly didn't understand the other things I'd spoken about. Although I had to admit that a portion of what he said was accurate, I sounded desperate, lonely, and lame.

As I sat glowering at Ken, Chris—a boy I'd noticed from day one for his serious demeanor that hid the most adorable face—got up to give his presentation. Dressed in what I'd soon learn was his school uniform of blue jeans, a white T-shirt, and hiking boots, Chris exuded a steely expression that made me sit up and take notice. There was something so contradictory about him: His eyes could be fixed and focused but twinkle with warmth and depth; he barely laughed out loud, but looked as though he held the potential for sidesplitting fun. He was everything Jonathon wasn't: clean-cut, conservative, and (gasp!) a Republican. But I also knew that he was smart, well read, and interested in having a dialogue that went beyond what kind of great bud got you so stoned that you could actually hallucinate. In class, the person who interviewed Chris didn't reveal any of these things, but I saw more in him. And I loved him at first sight.

"Do you want a piece of gum?" I asked Chris one day before class. I wanted to be wittier, but I also just wanted to find a reason to talk to him. "Sure," he said, smiling, and making me love him even more. By the end of class, we had plans to go to the library that evening to study and do some research for our next speech. When he came to pick me up, I was ready to go. I'd just worked out, but I figured that my sweatpants and beaten-up T-shirt were fine to study in. Chris, however, was freshly showered and wearing different clothes from the ones I'd seen him in that day. That's when I knew he liked me.

Somewhere between my block and the library, I reached over and held Chris's hand. The gesture had begun as sort of a joke, but he let my fingers stay entwined in his until we reached campus. We never did study for class that night—instead, we sat out on a bench in front of the library and talked. Then we went back to my apartment, ordered dinner, and talked some more. That conversation, over the span of just one night, made me feel so close to Chris. This was much more intimate than any sexual experience I'd encountered—it was as if our souls were meeting for the first time after a long period of separation.

There was an ease and acceptance in Chris that I'd been longing for, and an intelligence and challenge that kept me on my toes. We flirted mercilessly with each other, yet everything remained very nonsexual. I couldn't figure it out. I guessed we were becoming . . . friends.

All summer Chris and I were inseparable. There was an exhilaration I felt by having him in my life, and we had a connection and bond that I didn't know could exist between two people. I'd loved Jonathon, but this feeling was even deeper and more mature, and I wanted very much to take it the next level. I knew that Chris liked me, but I wondered if he was ever going to make a move. You see, he was older and in a period of self-imposed celibacy. He felt that even though he was 21, he didn't want to hook up with a woman unless he had feelings for her and felt they could have a relationship together. Surely that made him the weirdest 21-year-old on campus, but that's what I adored about Chris. He had such clear ideas about himself and his values and proved that to me over and over again.

One night, after a lot of laughter and stimulating dialogue, I leaned over to kiss him. He stopped me. Gently. I felt so embarrassed and couldn't believe that I'd misread him.

"Jess, I know you just got out of your relationship with Jonathon, and I like you too much to be a rebound," Chris said with a delicate strength. "You're not ready for a relationship yet, and I want to wait until it's right and you're ready."

My heart first filled with exuberance and gratitude for this man, and then it melted with intense love. He saw into me, too, and he loved what he saw. The incredible connection we shared finally did segue into a relationship, after more than a year. It was well worth the wait. I had some serious work to do on myself first.

Group Insanity

The mismatched chairs in our therapy room were assembled in the round. I liked to get there early to snag the comfy faded-pink chair with overstuffed cushions that I could dig my fingers into when things got particularly tense. No one could have warned me about the intensity of group therapy. It certainly wasn't what I expected, and I sometimes pondered why I was there. But I never felt as if I didn't fit in. Maybe I didn't cut myself or face a sexually abusive past, but I understood what it felt like to share such a distinct dislike of my being that I thought I could somehow control it.

You would have never known by sitting next to these women in class or passing them on the street that their lives held such tortured secrets. And I grew angrier and angrier that society wasn't talking about the stories I was hearing in group, or the experiences I'd had in my life so far. Everyone seemed to be sharing the same pain, yet no one was talking about it. Everyone had a story to tell, including me. Each semester there were eight of us in the eating-disorders group. At some point, one or two would inevitably drop out, and a solid six would remain. I was the only regular all four years. Our group was led by Pamela, a serene definition of a new-age hippie, complete with Birkenstock sandals; flowy, airy pants; tops with flowered prints; and a pashmina thrown delicately over her shoulders.

I loved two things about Pamela: her voice and her hands. Her voice had a lilt to it that begged us to open up and tell the truth. It covered our ears in a protective syrup of safety that felt both nurturing and motherly. And when she had something to express, her magnificent hands dodged, flowed, chopped, and swept the air to emphasize points of empathy and strength. Her fingernails were short and seemed to blend into her rosy fingers, which held a gold wedding band on her left ring finger and a silver-and-amethyst ring on her right thumb. She was in her late 40s, so her hands told of her age and experience through the wrinkles and folds. When I was lost for words or thoughts, I'd watch her hands and they seemed to coax me out of emotional hiding and lure me into painful truth.

All sessions began with silence, for no one ever knew how to start. But even during that quiet time, I could always tell that the hour would end up revealing tremendous stories that would elicit the growth of the women in this group. Our circles of silence could last up to ten minutes without a sound, and for some, the silence alone was the worst part. For women who struggle with eating disorders and addiction, sitting in silence can be more painful than the act of starvation and throwing up—because in the quiet, we hear our voices, the abuse, and the twisted thoughts. And we'd have to sit in that silence and feel the emotions that we'd been running from, hiding from, eating over, and starving away. We felt uncomfortable, and there was no coping behavior to cover it up. We had to sit there and feel until the first person broke the space with a word.

"Who wants to start?" Pamela asked.

On this particular Thursday, the air felt especially filled with angst and deeply buried pain. No one answered Pamela's question, and it felt as though we might just end up sitting there for the entire hour without saying a word. Finally, Pamela said, "Why don't you start, Jessica?" But today, I didn't know where to begin.

My eyes darted around the room for a sign of help. Everyone looked down at the floor except for Beth, who was picking away at the skin around her fingernails. Beth had many nervous habits that included twirling her hair until little clumps of it were yanked from her scalp, pulling the skin off around her cuticles so that you could see the bloodied traces of new skin run all the way down her fingers, and picking the scabs on her body until she had reached the core of her covered pain and made herself bleed again. She'd been diagnosed with obsessive-compulsive disorder (OCD) and was bulimic and anorexic. Beth had once been on our Big Ten gymnastics team until the coach deemed her behavior too "weird" and a "threat to the other team members," so she was kicked off the team.

The only person Beth was a threat to was herself. Beth had shared with us that she'd been violently raped by her brother for 14 years, and no one in her family knew about it. She finally broke the cycle of abuse by going out of state to college. She told us that she binged and purged to control the memory of the assault. She said she stuffed her face with food to numb the pain and then she'd throw up to release it. The oddest thing about Beth was that she always walked around with a smile. She'd grin, even as she was telling us the most horrendous story. She didn't ever cry, for she felt that if she started, she might never stop. She told us that she hadn't cried since the first night her brother raped her—when she cried, he'd thrust into her harder, so Beth learned to stifle her tears.

Sitting next to Beth was always Mary Ellen. First a drug addict before she transferred her addiction to anorexia, Mary Ellen's drug of choice was cocaine. She was introduced to it by her mother's boyfriend when she was 16; by the time she was 19, she'd racked up more than $24,000 worth of credit-card debt on shopping sprees she went on while coked up. She lived in the world of excess and bounced back and forth between shopping, using drugs, and bingeing.

In an effort to control her drug habit, Mary Ellen started to restrict her food intake. One affliction fueled another, and before she knew it she'd, whittled away to 89 pounds on a 5'10" frame. Mary Ellen had freckles that dotted her nose and continued down to her lips and chin. I never thought about a drug addict having freckles.

Then there was Alexis, the reason we were all so silent that day.

Alexis was a graduate student and a few years older than the rest of us. We looked to her for guidance, since she not only came to our group, but she'd also been in and out of hospitals for three or so years. In group, she often spoke first and seemed the strongest. Alexis lived with her mom and was known as a "townie." Even though she grew up in central Pennsylvania, she spoke with an affected British accent because she once spent a summer in England with her biological father. Something happened in that summer abroad that threw Alexis into a deep depression that was only soothed by having short, meaningless sexual affairs with older men.

I could tell by Pamela's questions that she thought Alexis had been abused by her father, but Alexis never copped to that. Instead, she'd make us laugh as she regaled us with tales of how she and her professors would make out in the faculty lounges and men's rest rooms on campus, barely escaping getting caught by other students. Even in her pain, Alexis couldn't hide her light—she glowed like a loving big sister whom we wanted to root for, even though we knew that she was hurting herself. Her sexuality and her binge eating were closely linked: When she was having an affair, she was highly restrictive with food; when she wasn't, she ate and ate until, as she said, "I could feel the food fill up to my eyeballs."

It took ten weeks for us to learn that Alexis was also a cutter. Intensely depressed when she wasn't taking an older lover, she'd slice into the skin on her thighs, hips, and underarms. Confessing that she often cut the word "HATE" into her flesh, she showed us the scabs and scars that she hid under long-sleeved shirts and sweatpants. And I think even Pamela was shocked to learn this.

Alexis would be the first one to hand someone a tissue when they cried in group or make sure they received a hug after an emotional release. Alexis was also the caregiver for her mother, who refused to work a steady job. Consequently, Alexis was in grad school and working full time while juggling men, binge eating, and mutilation.

Over the weekend before this session, word leaked out that Alexis had performed what she once called "the final cut": suicide. She bled to death. And she didn't leave a note.

"Jessica?" Pamela prodded again.

As I looked around at the group and noticed Alexis's empty chair, I just started to cry. And slowly, the others joined me. For at least 20 minutes, all that could be heard were faint sobs and sniffles from the downturned heads.

Pamela spent the remaining time trying to make some sense of what had happened to Alexis. "Why don't you go home and write down what you're feeling, what you were unable to say today, and we can start all over again next time," she told us. And with that, we all left without having said a single word.

Waking Up the World

Words poured out of my body and onto the page for eight straight hours. Piled high next to me were wadded-up tissues containing the tears and mucus of this emotional discharge. I left my body in a sense during this time, and what took over was a creative muse, a spiritual guide that let all of the voices I'd heard in my life just slide into a performance piece that I titled *Wake Up World.*

The piece was a messy configuration of monologues, poetry, scenes, dance, and music, peppered with slides of artwork and carrying forth messages dealing with political, social, and emotional issues. Within these 47 pages lay the experience of my 18 years on Earth. The stories in my life insinuated themselves into passages for the stage, and before I knew it, I'd convinced a group of friends (including my ex-boyfriend Jonathon) to participate in what would be my debut as a writer, director, and bearer of important stories.

For three weeks, we rehearsed these dense, angry, moving, and tragic pieces that explored relationships, drug abuse, eating disorders, abortion, censorship, language, and secrets. I wrote of all things political since it was 1992 and an election year. I wrote of Roy Avery; of Alexis, Josie, Laura, Mark, and Jonathon; of all of the tales I'd collected in group; and of snatches of conversation I'd heard while in motion on campus. Finally, these stories were going to be told.

We performed *Wake Up World* to a packed house of about 80 students in an underground space on campus called "Outlaws." It was a tiny black-box theater commandeered by the students and used to display original work. People pushed the envelope here, so it was a safe space to take a risk. Most performances didn't begin until 10 P.M., yet students would generally begin lining up as early as 8 o'clock to get a seat.

I thought I was going to die as the lights dimmed and my words, characters, and existence came to life before my eyes. I sat next to the light-board operator, carefully noting all of the audience's laughs, half-laughs, and incomplete laughs, as well as the sighs, moans, shifting of weight, coughs, and sniffles. I could barely manage to look anywhere but straight onstage because I couldn't believe that I was actually doing this—sharing so deeply yet so anonymously. The audience didn't know just how autobiographical this all was because they were also finding pieces of themselves in those stories. I spoke for myself that night *and* for the countless others who no longer had a voice.

I was delighted to hear the thunderous applause and hoots and hollers when the group took a final bow after concluding a moving nonverbal piece that used hand-painted signs to share messages of peace about the environment and the Persian Gulf War. I certainly didn't discriminate against any issue that night.

Then something strange happened. The play was over, people were clapping, the cast took their bows, and the lights slowly came back up . . . but no one moved. The clapping had died down, yet not a soul left their seat. They sat looking at the stage and the actors, many of whom had already headed backstage when they suddenly turned back around and noticed what I did.

A woman had her hand raised in the audience, and she kept it hanging there, waiting to be called on as if we were in class. "I have a question," she bellowed. "Can I ask the director a question?"

The entire cast turned to me, as did the audience, and I felt my eyes grow in size, as I had no idea what to expect next. *Shit, I thought, she hated it and she's going to tell me so in front of everyone!* Yet I moved through my fear to get onstage. I stood in front of the cast and said, "Go ahead. I'm the director—what's your question?"

"Well, it's more of a comment than a question, I guess. I . . . uh . . . you know how you had that one monologue where the girl threw up after what she ate?"

"Yes," I said.

"Well, I didn't know that was called *bulimia*. I just thought it was what girls did after they ate so they wouldn't get fat. My mom and sister always throw up after they eat, and I didn't know it had a name."

Some in the crowd gasped, some began to whisper, and another woman turned to her and said, "How could you not know? I watched my roommate do that all last year, and I think it's gross. Why do people do that?" Then she turned to me. "Why did you write that monologue?"

I began to answer her questions, and soon a dialogue erupted that ended up lasting longer than the play had. The cast answered questions about what it was like to perform their scenes, I answered questions about my motivation as a writer and creator, and the audience began to talk to each other and attempt to answer each other's questions. A spontaneous open conversation ensued, and it held within it debate, disagreement, confessions, and advice. I moderated it with pure instinct and intuition, and I made sure that the young woman who asked about bulimia left the room that night with the phone number for our counseling center.

The most beautiful part of the post-show discussion was that the audience, performers, and myself all took care of each other.

An offstage dance was ignited between giver and receiver, artist and patron, human being and human being. What was happening transcended a typical theatrical production—it flirted with being a classroom debate, a friendly chat, and a group therapy session. But all of it hinged on the pieces we put forth that night. We'd used art as a catalyst for discussion, and people were really talking! *There* was the dialogue I'd been craving, and the acknowledgment of important things out in the world.

I'd stumbled upon a whole new way to be an artist and human being. As an artist, I was in heaven knowing that my creations had spawned an experience that many felt had moved them enough to speak out loud. As a human being, I was honored that others respected, and resonated with, my thoughts and experiences. For a girl who had been so hungry for attention, acceptance, under-standing, love, peace, and connection, I was finally filled up in a way that I'd never imagined. And this wasn't some warped TV drama or afternoon talk show. Although I was still in college, I'd found the beginning of a career.

✳ ✳ ✳

chapter 6

The Mifflin Mob

The societal structure of college life is just a microcosm of the outside world. There are political issues, class systems, bureaucracies, agendas, secrets, and injustices that occur under the guise of "tradition." Since I attended a school that was the size of a small city, I was amazed that I could use my voice as profoundly as I had and still be heard. After discovering the power in performing socially relevant work with *Wake Up World,* I was hooked. I didn't have a clue as to how I'd make a living with it after college, but I knew that I had to continue creating pieces of work that opened up lines of communication and forced people to think. Once I started to speak out, it was hard to stop and be quiet again. The activist inside me was awakened.

As a freshman, I'd heard about the streaking tradition that overtook the campus during finals week of spring semester. It had originated in the '70s as a prank in one all-male dormitory, Mifflin Hall—four or five men had run naked through campus during finals, supposedly to relieve the pressure of studying. Over the years, however, this tradition had ballooned into an excuse for hundreds of men to run through campus (fully clothed now), destroying property while howling, chanting, and egging girls on to "show us your tits" or "take it off" in their dorm rooms. It was a loud, intimidating form of harassment that shut down campus on a spring night during finals week and sent a loud and clear message to women that they were nothing more than pieces of meat. Forget the fact that we were studying for our chemistry or art history tests—really all that mattered was that we strip in front of the windows and bare our breasts in order to feed the hungry mob outside our residence halls.

That there were women who ran with the mob mortified me. During my first year on campus, I was walking home from the library and got caught up in the sea of groping hands, hooting whistles, and mass hysteria. Before my R.A. pulled me into our hall, I turned to look back at the swarm of sweaty, robotlike students I'd squeezed through, and I noticed some women's faces in the group. They looked at me like I couldn't take a joke. But one person who especially didn't see the humor in this situation was a girl on our floor who had barricaded herself in the bathroom to escape the sexual taunts outside her window.

The chants had caused her to recall a gang rape that had happened in her hometown over Christmas break; consequently, she had a breakdown inside the bathroom stall. The university's response to this incident was to ask that all women refrain from using the rest rooms during the mob's activity. They came up with slogans such as "Pull the shade on harassment" and encouraged us to stay locked inside our rooms—completely ignoring the fact that the constant roar of voices made it impossible to relax or feel safe, even while barricaded in our own rooms.

I engaged in traditional activist duties such as protests, letter writings, and candlelight vigils for the next three years, yet the tradition continued. Then, in my senior year, a fellow student informed me of a program on MTV called MTV News Unfiltered. Their purpose was to expose real-life news stories through the eyes of Generation X. The show had a toll-free number for story ideas, and I managed to get through to make an impassioned pitch about the "institutionalized sexual harassment" at my university. I told the person on the phone about the shameful imprisonment of women inside their dorm rooms while the mostly male mob ran amuck on campus. The next thing I knew, I was figuring out how to use the two handheld cameras that MTV had sent me to shoot this story.

Getting any kind of student support seemed nearly impossible, unless I was crusading for free coffee on campus or more student parking. Asking students to take a moment out of their congested days to speak up and voice their disgust at a tradition that sexually terrorized women seemed almost laughable. In fact, laughter is the first response I got from most students when I polled them in the dining halls about the Mifflin Mob.

"It's no big deal—it happens one night," was the standard response from most people. And they told me this while they scooted away, afraid to catch the dreaded "activist's disease." Then there were those students who related amazing horror stories of being harassed or assaulted by the mob, but when asked if they'd lend their faces and voices to the cause, they declined for fear of retribution—which had actually been the case when some others on campus had been involved in a protest. I understood, for I'd lived through the event.

During my third year of school, a bunch of us had gotten together to hold a candlelight vigil right at the opening of Mifflin Hall, where the mob originated. We may have been only 40 strong—and we were peaceful women, gay men, and one brave faculty member—but we spread out across the threshold of Mifflin Hall and made our union known. The police had been there all night urging us to go home, ignoring the fact that a swarm of misguided students had just destroyed thousands of dollars' worth of property on campus. Apparently the real nuisance was the 40 of us praying and holding a space for change.

There were about *600 people* running in the mob that night, and when they came upon us, we had one of those intense staredowns reminiscent of an old Western. Some nasty remarks were thrown our way, and in proper, nonviolent form, we held on to each other's hands a bit tighter and made sure that our candles didn't blow out.

Then it happened.

Without warning, some of the men tried to rush through our ring. Suddenly we were caught with our bodies wide open—we were vulnerable because of our commitment to holding hands and carrying candles. They ripped through the group, punching many of us in the stomach, pushing others to the ground, and never missing a chance to spew forth degrading language in the process. I felt a sharp jab in my gut and lost sight of where my candle and fellow hand-holder had gone.

The entire confrontation was quick, frightening, and over within few minutes. The police didn't do much to break it up—in fact, they employed a scolding tone with *us,* as though we'd somehow asked to be hit and assaulted.

Chris came to meet me afterwards, and he looked as though he were collecting a soldier coming home from a war. He was solemn and reserved, and quietly put his arm around me as we walked back to his dorm. I tried to get him to join in the protest with me, but he refused. He disagreed with my opinion that the mob was a horrible thing—I'd even discovered the night before that Chris had run with the mob his freshman year. To him, it was no big deal, a rite of passage for young men on campus.

In the past, our intellectual debates seemed enjoyable and even tinged with ease when we stood on opposite sides of the political- and social-issue fence. But this one really hurt. For my boyfriend not to support me, or understand why I felt the mob was so wrong, made me question my voice and feel uncertain for using it.

As a result of this experience, I came to understand that there were some people who would never think of taking a stand in public. Chris felt that his opinion was his own, not to be expressed to the world. I didn't understand how he could sit by and let an injustice happen in front of his eyes. He blamed it on gender differences; I blamed it on passion. The end result was that I slept with one eye open that night, not sure whom to trust or how to feel. And as I thought about how I'd been physically assaulted, I reminded myself that the last time I'd felt a blow like that was with Mark, and I'd vowed never to be hit again. But with Mark, I had denied my anger and right to feel violated. Tonight was different. I was mad— and I set out to get even.

MTV and the Absent Mob

During my senior year, people were definitely tuned in to the fact that MTV was going to cover this story. In the days leading up to the running of the mob, I'd endured death threats, rape threats, and even a threat to withhold my diploma should I go through with this "media experiment." But, armed with the support of a national cable network, I was finally able to find about 100 supporters who were unafraid to show their faces. I sent one woman with a camera inside the residence hall to document the oppressive messages sent to women that night. The university had actually issued official posters using the slogan "Pull the shade on harassment," and women were told to hang them in the windows for the screaming men to see. This was our school's form of protest—a preprinted sign that essentially said, "The woman behind the window doesn't approve of your behavior and wants no part of it." Well, that was too damn saccharine for me. I wanted to shine a light on this intimidation, and there was no better way to get an administration's attention than to draw the media into it.

At 8:00 P.M., our group set up shop in front of the cluster of female residence halls, assembling into a shape that resembled a heart more than a circle. We held a prayer ceremony and candlelight vigil, along with a speak-out for those who wished to share their opinions with the group and the camera. Some spoke of being assaulted and harassed during the running of the Mifflin Mob, while many felt that this kind of excused behavior—the "boys will be boys" mentality—was the exact kind of misogynistic practice in our society that keeps women silent when they're hurt and keeps men believing that it's "no big deal."

We were in direct contact with an undercover reporter in one of the women's residence halls, and we'd even landed a coup: A fraternity brother who lived in Mifflin Hall had agreed to radio us when the mob started so that we'd be sure to capture it on camera. Many in our group didn't trust the motivations of this man, but I did. He'd confided to me that his girlfriend had been raped in high school, and she'd explained to him how these men being allowed to treat women in such a disrespectful way only further set the stage for an unsafe atmosphere.

The quiet sky released a drizzle as we waited for the mob to run, and the slogans on the signs that people had created—such as "Enough is Enough" and "No More Mob"—began to melt down and blend on the colorful posterboard backgrounds. And then we heard some high-pitched hoots and hollers coming from inside one of the female dorms.

We looked up, and peeking out from behind the university-issued window coverings were a bunch of women who began to scream, "Thank you! Thank you for protecting us!" A few more joined in, and soon we were serenaded by women's voices, thanking us for being there and standing in the rain to protect their rights. Many yelled their words of gratitude, but I also noticed the women who just watched from their rooms and gave silent approval with a thumbs-up or a faint smile of relief.

It was nearing 10:00 P.M., and in years past, the mob would have been in full swing by now. Our source from Mifflin Hall said that he hadn't heard a thing all night, which was really weird. Surely the brazen beings who had charged and assaulted people the year before wouldn't be deterred by a little drizzle and some cameras. Yet, by the time 11:00 rolled around, we'd been out protesting for three hours. Then we got word that the mob had started on the other end of campus, near the engineering and science buildings. We waited and listened, for usually the echoes of chanting voices could be heard for minutes before the masses appeared. We didn't hear anything. Now it was midnight, and we all had the same feeling: Even those most committed to tearing up a little campus that night would have surely gotten started by now.

We called their bluff and waited until 12:30 A.M., at which point, our group of rain-soaked and exhausted protesters retired to our rooms or homes in complete amazement. For the first time in years, the mob didn't run. It was no longer fun for these people, since they ran the risk of being caught on camera—and in a way that wouldn't exactly make Mom and Dad proud.

We'd stopped a decades-long tradition, simply by using our will, our voices, and our cameras. I was hooked on the power of the media. MTV, however, didn't share my enthusiasm for the fact that the Mifflin Mob had failed to show up at its own party. "It doesn't make good TV, Jessica," an executive producer said. "I mean, it's great that you stopped the tradition and everything, but we need to show people *what* you stopped." So, with some help from the archives of local TV stations and newspapers, we located footage that showed the mob going to town long before I was even a student.

Next, I was told: "Turn the camera toward yourself and tell America why you did what you did."

I looked into the lens, and after cracking up for the first couple of takes, I managed to share how I'd taken a stand so that people would know it wasn't okay to oppress others. But the truth was, I didn't really know *why* I'd done it.

Certainly the old Jessica would never have taken such a public stand, where she ran such a risk of being ridiculed, picked on, and hated again. Yet my experience as a woman so far had told me that if I didn't do *something*, I'd have to live with the consequences of a world that told women to stay inside, be quiet, and never forget that in the end, we're just sexual objects. That just wasn't acceptable for me.

CNN and the Already-Dead Girl

My swan song at Penn State was an original play I helped to create, entitled *Body Loathing, Body Love*. A poetic blend of monologue, dance, slides, performance art, and abstract improvisation, this piece summed up the intense battle I'd had with my eating disorder. Because the piece was so personal, I was going to moderate the audience discussion that by now had become an integral part of my work.

The evening *Body Loathing, Body Love* was performed, we crammed more than 200 people into a common room inside one of the residence halls. It would be my last show before I graduated, and everyone I'd fallen in love with (and fallen apart with) in my therapy group was there. This was going to be my chance to truthfully talk about all the journeys, whispers, cries, screams, and howls that we'd shared.

In the audience, along with scores of searching faces, was a camera crew from CNN. They had originally come to campus to do a story on eating disorders in college sports, yet their interview subject's coach had decided to pull her involvement from the piece for fear of bad press for the team. However, my counselors and theater staff had suggested that the camera crew come check out the show. So now I had three cameras witnessing what would become my most memorable experience in college.

The play itself went off without a hitch. Following our curtain call, our dialogue began. At first it was shaky, as the students sitting on the couches and floors pretended to ignore the cameras moving inches away from their faces as they spoke. This was a time when reality TV was just beginning. MTV's *The Real World* was in its first season, and *Survivor, The Osbournes,* and *American Idol* were years away—we were just beginning to taste the art-imitates-life programs that are now a part of our daily diet.

The bravery in the room that night took form in the candid stories that this group of students agreed to share. I was in heaven as our discussion moved effortlessly from social opinion to debate to cathartic personal story.

Then the girl in the last chair on the left raised her hand to speak. I knew she was going to respond to the question that had just been posed. A guy had asked how somebody's supposed to know when another person needs help, and his words had been loaded with the heaviness of someone whose attempts at rescuing a friend were futile. The young woman told him, "Sometimes you won't know. Sometimes they're in so much pain that the words can't come out of their mouth."

People began craning their necks to look at her because her voice was trembling so much. The CNN crew honed in on her, and a boom mike floated on top of her head to pick up her sound.

She fearlessly continued, "I tried reaching out to my friends my first year of school here, and no one seemed to get it. They all thought I had it together and was perfectly in control. The only thing I was in control of was how many times I tried to commit suicide, yet nothing worked. I was throwing up at least ten times a day, and at the same time making straight A's. No one thought I had a problem."

For some reason, I thought this girl looked vaguely familiar, so I peered closer at her. She went on: "I felt that no one was listening to me, so one day, after I'd thrown up for like the millionth time that day, I saw one of those posters in the bathroom that warned about the dangers of eating disorders. It said you could die from it, and that made me so angry. So I went back to my room to get a black marker, and I came back into the bathroom and wrote on it, 'FUCK YOU, I'M ALREADY DEAD.'"

Oh my God—it was her.

I noticed that the girls in the front row were crying with connection. My stomach gurgled and felt warm with the intensity in the room. For some reason, the girl had looked at me the whole time she spoke and I finally realized that the woman who had opened up her heart for the world to see was Amy, from my freshman dorm.

At the end of the program, she approached me, and even though her hair was shorter and not so blonde, I instantly remembered her defiant ponytail and rock-hard demeanor. The woman who stood before me was softer, fuller, and in uncontrollable pain. I hugged her, as the cameras zoomed in. I felt the microphone pack press up against my back as I squeezed her even tighter.

Amy told me that she'd gone into treatment the summer after our freshman year and had just returned to school that spring. She'd cut off her ponytail because it reminded her of the old Amy—she wanted to forget that girl.

I didn't really know Amy, except for that one time in the bathroom and all of the gossip about her perfect life. But she knew me. She said she was proud of me, and I stopped cold. "Why?" I asked.

"Because," she said, "you're making a difference and shining a light on this darkness."

Amy was the most familiar stranger I'd ever known, one who carried a message that I'd hear again and again. I'd let that message guide me into the next phase of my life.

✻ ✻ ✻

chapter 7

Heading Midwest

"W̲hy don't you move in with Chris?"

My mother had just handed me the greatest out from really facing life after graduation. At the time, the idea of moving with Chris to Indianapolis, where he had a job, seemed so much better than going to New York, which now held zero passion for me since I no longer wanted to be a leading lady. And Los Angeles had long been out of the question—I did not want to get involved in an industry that was hell-bent on destroying images of women by emphasizing and promoting their body parts, like oversexed blue-plate specials.

No, what I wanted to do emerged for me once I landed in the middle of suburban domestic bliss, playing house with Chris in Indianapolis. I'd never thought I would actually live in the Midwest, and I feared there would be a shortage of social issues to tackle—I was certain that everyone would be white bread, happy, and extremely conservative. In reality, this town proved to be the birthplace of my career, holding many opportunities for me. It was like a beach that had never been walked on, and I was soon able to see my original footprints in the sand.

Emily and Size-14 Therapy

My first job was at a women's clothing store in a mall near our new apartment. I needed something to get me out of the house as I made the uncomfortable adjustment to being Chris's "romantic roommate." Living together post-college without the bonds of marriage was much more difficult than I'd imagined. While our love for each other was undeniable, at our core, Chris and I were two very different people.

I knew that he truly didn't understand why I chose to live my life out loud and for everyone to see. And our different political and social views were never remedied—instead, we just swept them under the rug. We lived for quite some time in that in-between place of being monogamously committed but not ready for marriage. We lied and told people that we were engaged, but the truth was that we didn't know *what* we were. We were just holding on.

I was excited about my first day of work. I thought I'd enjoy it, mostly because of the discounts. What I found was that my natural inclination to help women heal would even follow me here. I was a good salesperson because I loved talking to people, and I loved clothes. I also understood the plight of the average American female shopper, who's forced to undergo wiggling, pulling, and zipping in front of a stark mirror lit by glaringly tacky fluorescent lights. *No one* looks good under these lights, especially curvier girls. These mirrors just seem cruelly designed to capture and accentuate every little bulge or roll—I often heard heavy breathing and sighing coming from outside the dressing room where I stood guard.

On the day I met Emily and her mother, I was having a great day, since two teenagers who were shopping for back-to-school clothes had remembered me from the MTV piece. It was the summer after our Mifflin Mob victory, and MTV kept repeating the show, since I guess it got decent ratings. I couldn't believe that all the way in Indiana, I was a pseudo-celebrity.

Riding pretty high off that recognition, I began to daydream about what else I wanted to do besides get people a larger or smaller size. Then Emily's mother approached me and asked for some help in getting her daughter geared up for her first semester away at college, which was commencing in a week.

I asked to see Emily to determine what size she wore, and her mother whispered, "Emily won't come out of the dressing room because she thinks she's too fat."

I went in to see this young girl, who was sort of perching on the tiny dressing-room bench, holding a slew of tank tops in her hands. She looked mortified and defeated, and said, "I can't find anything to fit me. I'm too—"

Before she could call herself another ugly word, I jumped in: "Let me see what I can do." And off I zoomed to save Emily from herself and another bad shopping experience.

I *so* felt her pain—she wanted to be hip and trendy for her new college experience, yet every article of clothing she chose was designed for someone else's body. Since we were roughly the same size, a 14, I just went about the store collecting pieces that I'd personally wear. I reminded myself that we all should find clothes that fit our bodies, not mangle our bodies to fit into clothes.

I returned with a bundle of fall wardrobe options and stepped outside the fitting room as Emily began to try things on.

"I would never wear this stuff!" she said, as I crossed my fingers and hoped I didn't urge her into another breakdown.

"Just try them on," I said. "I think you need to change your idea of what to wear so that you can pick clothes that make you feel strong and not stuffed into something not made for you."

Several minutes later, Emily called me in. She had on a pair of dark brown jeans and a creamy sweater—and she looked radiant. After Emily had stared at herself in the mirror as if meeting a stranger for the first time, she slid down the wall and onto the crumpled pile of previously tried-on clothes, and started to cry.

Her mom popped her head in to see what was going on. I thought for sure that I was going to get fired because I was making a customer cry. "What's wrong, honey?" Emily's mom asked.

"Nothing, Mom. I actually feel pretty."

I exhaled and silently thanked God, as Emily asked, "How did you know what to get me?"

I answered, "Well, I know what it's like to go shopping when you have boobs, a butt, and a curvy belly. I'm learning that I have to surrender the notion that I can wear anything a size-2 can wear. And I'm learning to shop for my body type so that I don't have to feel defeated every time I get dressed. I just did the same for you."

Emily explained that she'd gone on an antidepressant that made her gain a lot of weight, and she was so uncomfortable in her new skin that she'd avoided going shopping for more than a year—instead, she usually ordered through catalogs.

For the next half hour, Emily and I talked about her fears: from starting college and being away from home, to handling the stress of school, to trying to get a handle on her depression. Once you broke it down, her body image and clothing size really weren't at the top of her list of grievances—she had much deeper emotions running through her.

I completely saw myself in Emily, and truly could have cared less if she bought anything. I was just so glad to have made a connection to another young woman. But in the end, Emily and her mother bought more than $1,000 worth of back-to-school clothes from me. Within weeks, I received letters from headquarters asking me to consider becoming a manager. It seems that Emily and her mother had both written evaluation letters to the corporate office, extolling my compassion and empathy for Emily. My bosses thought it was a sales technique, but I knew better.

I soon quit selling clothes to pursue my calling full time.

Youth and the Arts

"I did it!" I exclaimed as I threw my bag on the couch and woke Chris up from a nap. In my hands I held a check for $5,000, the result of an all-day grant-writing course that I'd taken at our local community college.

I'd enrolled in the class to figure out how to start my own theater company, since I'd beaten down the doors of every theater in Indianapolis and none of them had expressed any interest in creating a social-issues theater company for young people. Apparently children's theater should only include tired old fairy tales with overemphasized moral lessons that simply don't resonate with anyone over the age of five.

All those nos drove me to create a company that had a similar structure to the one I was a part of in college. On the mission statement I had to create, I boldly announced that we'd operate as both a training academy for the arts and a traveling repertory company creating interactive theater for kids ages 12 to 24.

In order to be eligible for grants funding, I needed to have nonprofit status (which I didn't have), and my company had to have been in existence for at least three years. Such a catch-22! So I found a local cabaret-style theater whose audience was primarily of the generation who longed to hear more Hoagy Carmichael songs, and I persuaded them to let me run my company out of their basement. I borrowed their nonprofit number, and I was off.

I was 21 years old and had no idea how to run a company, but I knew that $5,000 could really start the ball running. I mostly just let my guidance and intuition run loose. The first thing I did was create a summer theater program, which offered free classes in the areas of theater, dance, and music to at-risk youth. My first outreach program was based on the beautiful and expensive summer arts academies I'd had the luxury of attending as a young girl. My parents had spent thousands of dollars to give me the opportunity to play, paint, sing, dance, create magical characters, and cultivate rich friendships. I had no idea at the time that they'd given me such a gift—but now I wanted to give a similar gift to kids less fortunate than I was.

What had intrigued me most about creating this summer program was the social experiment I wanted to manifest. I wanted to take kids from the suburbs of Indianapolis and bring them together with urban youth. I wanted to blend the privileged worlds of those who could afford this camp with the worlds who didn't even know this kind of summer magic existed. And I wanted to offer it *for free.*

The label of "at risk" seems to conjure up images of poor, minority kids living in the "hood." *All* of this country's children are essentially at risk, even those "privileged" ones living in ivory towers on the outskirts of town. In the end, the arts can free the spirit of a trapped child and open up doors to communication, empowerment, and self-esteem, which every young person deserves. So, with these intentions, the Youth and the Arts summer program was born. The first year, only 12 young people were registered, but throughout the next five years, the program ballooned into an organization with 40 participants and double that amount on a waiting list to get in.

I made sure that our structure was loose enough to feel empowering, yet strong enough to feel loving. The students had their say with this program: Classes were structured with a built-in time for relaxation, meditation, or group feedback between teachers and students. Young people who had never tapped in to their creative potential eagerly arrived each morning before nine o'clock to catch a breakfast snack and then work on their murals, monologues, or dance routines.

At the end of each summer, we'd present a special performance night for family and friends that celebrated what we'd accomplished. We'd take an existing piece of material, such as *West Side Story,* and have the students update the general storyline with themes that were occurring in their lives. So *West Side Story* became *Indy Side Story,* and instead of a Puerto Rican and American influence, the kids chose a more abstract route and picked colors (red and blue) to represent the two different families. And instead of Tony dying at the end of the show, they created a big gang war that takes the lives of *both* lovers and their families, which was more realistic in their eyes. There wasn't a right or wrong here—the show was theirs to create and re-create in their own language and flair. To see the huge smiles on the faces of parents who had never been to a theatrical production before or even dreamed of seeing their child onstage was prize enough for me.

What was magical about this program was the transformation of a human being that the staff and I often witnessed in a few short weeks. For example, Annabelle was too petrified to walk across the stage when she first arrived for the summer program several years before. In an improvisation class, she was asked to walk across the stage as an emotion: happy, sad, and so forth. She couldn't even pick up her head as she shuffled along the stage. Her self-esteem had plummeted after her abortion, which had taken place when she was 13. She then began cutting herself regularly to punish herself for giving up her unborn child. Her mother and father wanted to commit her to a hospital, yet for some reason she ended up enrolled in my program. Slowly but surely, Annabelle made friends and picked up her head, and she was moving confidently by year two. By year three, she was readily raising her hand in classes and sharing her ideas. In year four, she came back as a counselor to help other students. Then, by year five, she was gracing the stage in a lead role that required her to experience *all* emotions, while singing, dancing, and acting her way across the stage. She did it brilliantly, and the audience gave her a standing ovation.

Marvin was a young man who many had written off for his volatile temper and foul mouth—he could use words that stung like pebbles from a slingshot. His father, who was very up front with me when I met him, said that we should feel free to discipline his son as we saw fit. It wasn't too long before I discovered that Marvin couldn't sit properly on the bike he rode to class because his father "disciplined" him with a belt so often. In turn, Marvin unleashed his rage on his peers and teachers. I had two teachers threaten to quit because of Marvin and his antics, but then I did something that surprised everyone. I gave Marvin a chance to be a counselor and make some money.

Many teachers thought I was idiotic to reward Marvin for his behavior and lack of interest by giving him a position many of the better students coveted and perhaps deserved. But I'd noticed something else about Marvin—he kept journals and loved to write, but only did it when his friends weren't around. Marvin had even let me read one of his entries. It was a poem about his dad, and he spoke of bloodied hands and broken hearts, and of the silent screams he cried for a dad who didn't beat him, for a dad who would remember to say good morning.

Marvin turned out to be an excellent counselor, and I also encouraged him to help us write the script for the new end-of-summer show. What emerged four weeks later was a show-stopping hip-hop and poetry jam/monologue that he delivered with such energy that it brought the house down.

Marvin shone brighter than anything I'd ever seen that night. His dad didn't come to the performance, but someone else was there. Denise, whose nephew was a new student in our program, was visiting from Washington, D.C., where she worked in the admissions office at a major university. Denise helped Marvin get a full scholarship to Georgetown University that fall, where he went on to study English and music.

The A.C.T. OUT Ensemble

I moved from one project to another with great ease, since being an entrepreneur and businesswoman fit me. I canvassed drama classes and undergraduate programs to find actors to audition for my new company, the A.C.T. OUT Ensemble. The first year, response was slim, but I did manage to pull together a company of four men and four women, ranging in age from 19 to 40. Most were community theater performers or students who had dropped out of school to work a semester before going back. The talent levels of the company weren't uniform—some were seasoned pros while others had never gotten paid for performing. And it wasn't like I was spoiling them with riches: I think the first year I was able to pay my actors $11 a show plus meals, which usually meant dinner rolls or some other food item that didn't go stale right away.

We did nine shows that season, and most of those gigs I booked by making appearances at local and national eating-disorder or student-activism conferences. My work with MTV and CNN had garnered me some invites to speak, and I'd incorporate my actors by splitting my presentation into two parts. First, they'd perform a 20- or 30-minute sketch about the subject matter, and then I'd come out and facilitate a dialogue with the audience about what they'd just seen. This event juiced up the typical feel of these conferences, and soon we were being asked to perform more than 100 times a year.

At first, we just traveled throughout the Midwest, hitting Indiana, Illinois, Ohio, and Michigan. By the end of our second year, we were getting booked simply through word of mouth. I never formally advertised our services (and looking back now, that amazes me)—we just seemed to always be right where we needed to be. Schools and community groups have a great networking system, so when we did a good job, I just asked that they pass on the word. We eventually grew into a nationally recognized company that traveled to almost half of the United States from 1995 to 2001. I don't think it could have worked out better if I had planned it.

The performers and I ended up using a kind of shorthand that only a traveling troupe can understand. Living together on the road, we knew all too well each other's eating and sleeping patterns, bathroom habits, and personal-hygiene downfalls. Made-up songs, stories, and jokes accompanied us as we drove early in the morning from town to town after a gig. The actors in my company followed my dream and theirs—and sacrificed comfort along the way.

We slept on cots in school infirmaries when our sponsors didn't have enough money to put us up in a hotel. When I was first learning to ration my company expenses on the road, we ate bagels for a week. We spent hours in a car to go to little Podunk towns across America that desperately needed a program about AIDS or teen pregnancy. The actors put up with my foibles as a leader, and they had the integrity and strength I could call on when I needed to. Every person who traveled with me on this journey changed and grew as a creative artist. But the best part of all was that we became better people. These beautiful human beings appeared for all different reasons in my life and were as drawn to this work as I was—we all wanted to heal our own demons and give back to the world.

Our shows provided audiences with the opportunity to get involved and be heard. Since I wasn't a psychotherapist or a medical doctor, I had the leeway to come at these issues from an emotional and theatrical level. I thrived off of exposing the underbelly of society and digging up what we weren't talking about. I used whatever means I had to get the point across—sometimes employing the contemporary dramatic structure of a one-act play; other times using slides, dance, performance art, or spoken word to evoke a particular feeling. The actors and I created pieces of story that drove our audience to respond by leaving the outcome of the characters open-ended, just like in real life. The actors sometimes stayed in character (as we'd experimented with in college) and would share a dialogue with the audience.

We covered topics including eating disorders, drug and alcohol abuse, and date rape at first, and then later added in shows on school violence, child abuse, diversity, homophobia, and hate crimes. Our work was almost always inspired by current news stories. I also wrote plays-on-demand for communities who were facing crises such as gang rapes, murder/suicides, or school shootings. And I always had a professional on hand to handle the really heavy stuff.

The A.C.T. OUT Ensemble used art as a catalyst for discussion and healing, and it was raw, organic, and unpolished. And because we had to travel from school to school and town to town, we had to be economical and practical with our sets and costumes. We remedied the costume issue by wearing black T-shirts that bore our company's name. If a particular role demanded a more specific costume, we'd add a hat, scarf, glasses, or jacket as needed—but our black T–shirts and black slacks became our company uniform.

Chris and his father helped me build my first set, which was made from PVC pipes and could be collapsed and constructed in a matter of minutes. The long, white piping fit together to form the outline of a 6' x 8' theatrical flat that we covered with a piece of black nylon. When we wanted to show slides or videos, we could interchange the black coverings for a white one. We carried the collapsed set in a giant ski bag, and also lugged a portable CD player, a slide projector, and a few props with us. We were our own stagehands and technicians, as our performances often took place in school cafeterias, auditoriums, or gymnasiums; office buildings; churches; or even hallways and stairwells.

We used postmodern conventions in theater, such as turning around when finished with a scene, or doing a two-person scene with the actors back-to-back when there wasn't enough room to move onstage, which was often the case. Our routines were limited, but we got immensely creative with using objects such as desks, chairs, blackboards, and stools to create levels and platforms upon which to move our bodies.

Many times our audience would begin no more than four feet away from the stage, so our actors developed intense discipline and concentration in maintaining the "fourth wall" (that is, the one closest to the audience, which separates the performers from them) because inevitably those that sat so close would talk, giggle, and just plain gossip about the appearance of a performer. To perform in front of more than 500 junior high or high school kids is to know what it's like to be heckled. We couldn't do this work and expect not to be. After all, we were coming into an unknown school at an ungodly hour to open kids' minds to the perils of drug and alcohol use in a way that couldn't preach or pander or else we'd be finished! Consequently, our challenge was to spew out enough information to make the audience think, react, and stick around to ask questions . . . all in an hour's time. We weren't solving any problems at these schools—we were merely opening up future communication to take place within their communities once we left. Like pied pipers, we flowed in and out of towns, leading young people to action and outreach. That was our job, and I wouldn't have had it any other way.

Out of financial necessity, sheer ignorance, and fortitude, I not only wrote the material, hired the actors, ran the rehearsals, directed the pieces, and facilitated the post-performance dialogue, but I also performed in some shows, booked all of our appearances, created our marketing materials, and somehow managed to get us featured in major newspapers such as *The Washington Post* and magazines like *Teen People*. Working in the nonprofit sector trains one to be efficient, creative, and resourceful on very limited and non-guaranteed funds. Fortunately for me, I didn't know any better, so I took on each job with a voracious appetite for survival—and I thrived on the results. I felt more alive putting together and running this company than I'd ever felt performing someone else's words.

I learned some very hard lessons about how to be a leader and a manager—for example, over the course of one season, I hired and fired more than 30 actors. Slowly I understood that I had to build a strong team of people around me, and I was learning that all-important word in business: *no*. For the first few years, I accepted jobs for free or with impossible working conditions because that's what I had to do to get my new company off the ground and get our name out there. But after a while, I learned to set boundaries and establish goals and working conditions that I just wouldn't budge from. Saying no can be the most empowering thing you do in business—and in your life—because when you refuse what's wrong for you, it opens up the opportunities for what's *right* to come rushing in.

To say I took my work home with me would be an understatement. People got stirred up when they saw the truth presented before them, and they really wanted to talk about it. It constantly amazed me to see how hungry folks were for a few minutes of uninterrupted time for them to spew. Whether they wanted to share confessions, longings, or even criticism, people needed a space to talk. I had to figure out how to listen and try not to heal and fix every person I met. At first I was horrible at it—I took every emotional outburst I witnessed during a performance home with me. I'd dream about the people I'd meet, worry for them, and feel personally responsible for their safety. Looking out into the faces of 500 eighth graders in Idaho or 20 college students in Pittsburgh, I saw the same thing: fear, denial, pain, anger, hope, lust, longing, confusion, confidence, and trust.

To think that in 60 minutes of time you can touch a life is awe-inspiring. I kept hearing the same stories from town to town, and it told me one thing—I was meant to be doing what I was doing. As imperfect, frenetic, and messy as it sometimes was, I was right where I needed to be.

A Slow Breaking Down

I opened the door to a clean apartment that smelled like fresh air and pine trees. The V-shaped lines on the carpet told me that Chris had just finished vacuuming before coming to get me at the airport. He always cleaned the apartment right before I came home from being on the road—it was his way of showing his love for me. But today I barely recognized it. Instead, I was busy focusing on everything else we were experiencing: intense arguing, yelling, my being on the road so much, nights spent in separate rooms watching TV when I *was* home, emotionally absent lovemaking sessions, and lots of sadness creeping in. I was feeling the slow breaking down of our relationship. I was consumed with work *and* consumed with the new me emerging. The similarities that had bonded Chris and me together in the beginning, along with the dire neediness from both of us to be loved, was being replaced (on my part) with a strong self-confidence and a desire for a more ambitious partner.

Chris had a brilliant mind, and he spent a lot of time in it, logically plotting his life to the point of paralyzing himself with inactivity. He sought work in the scientific field he had majored in while in college, but he was miserable with that decision. Chris was full of so many glorious possibilities, yet he was terrified to move away from science and admit he was in process. I begged him to follow what made his heart leap, and he finally did. Yet to admit that he didn't quite know what he wanted to do with his life was almost blasphemy in his family. He came from a long line of men who worked out of duty and not necessarily fulfillment or enjoyment. In contrast, I knew that watching my growth and success was hard for him. I was moving into my power, taking risks, and really taking off in all sorts of ways, and we were growing apart.

There were desperate attempts to stay connected by going to spiritual outings, mostly against his will, and by spending long weekends in the country with his family, mostly against my will. We were working so hard to change each other into what we wanted the other to be that we missed the beauty of who we were. And it got really dark before it was over.

For almost five years, I'd had the behavioral symptoms of my eating disorder under control. I no longer starved and binged and exercised in the excessive cycles of my youth. I knew too much now—I knew that I couldn't numb out to the world by eating or not eating. I recognized emotions when I experienced them and let them flow easily. Chris had a nickname for me: "Cries Too Much," fashioned after the names in the movie *Dances with Wolves.*

It's true. I cried all the time and felt so deeply. Going into recovery for my eating disorder caused me to learn how to feel all over again. I recognized just how much I repressed even everyday emotions. When I was little, I learned how to quell my emotions with food and exercise—now I was learning how to juggle a fuller life, one that came with a career that I was building, and a relationship I was responsible for.

Compulsive overeating, anorexia, and bulimia are progressive diseases, and the recovery process is continual and constant. While I was rid of most of my early destructive behaviors, I was still uncovering the reasons behind why I destroyed my body and spirit. As I talked to other people about this subject on the road, I thought I had to be cured, fixed, and solved. I thought I had to be the teacher and that meant that I was finished learning. I thought I had to be perfect. But the empty boxes and bags of food I consumed while traveling only showed me that I couldn't control myself and was a big phony. I'd come back to my hotel room after an emotional night of performing and facilitating—oftentimes after being repeatedly told "You saved my life tonight"—and order room service before processing how I felt. I'd eat over the tears I saw in the eyes of a father whose daughter was struggling with cutting herself, or I'd eat over a young woman's admission that she had been raped. It never got easier to hear those tales. And if I wasn't eating, I was going the opposite direction—restricting my food intake.

The strain of leaving Chris for periods of time, coupled with the many unforeseen emotional experiences, highs and lows, and everyday responsibilities while traveling on the road, led me to devise a way to feel more in control. Many a touring season saw me traveling with my special mugs of fresh juices, which were designed to clean me out during a 30-day fast. I bounced back and forth between restricting and bingeing as coping tools for being out in the world and doing a job that I loved. That showed me that not just depressed people struggle with this addiction. I ate (or didn't) over all shapes and sizes of feelings. I ate when I was successful, and I starved when I wasn't. I used my dis-ease to help digest the heartbreaking stories I was witness to. And sometimes I simply couldn't handle my own power and the change that was taking place inside of me.

When I first met Chris, I was a shell of the woman I was becoming. But did I have the strength to leave him *and* the old me behind? I was relapsing, yet I didn't seek help because I thought everything I'd worked for would be taken away from me. I thought for sure that the people who said I helped them would hate me because I was still struggling. What would people think? What would happen if they found out I was . . . human?

Moving Forward

I experienced such magnificent triumphs as my company grew and gained national recognition—I glimpsed pieces of a life I wanted, a life I was creating. Chris and I ended up staying together for seven and a half years. At the base of our relationship was an intense friendship formed in our youth, but which struggled to survive in our 20s. I didn't want to live in Indiana anymore. I wanted to take my work to the next level, so I decided to pursue a career in Los Angeles. I thought about doing TV and reaching my audience in a bigger, different format. I felt so saturated with the words I heard from young people as I traveled the country. Intensely driven to help share their stories from bigger platforms, I knew I needed to move forward. Figuring out how to do that felt impossible. It seems easy to spout cute slogans like "Just Do It," but the practical application of changing one's life is not neatly packaged in 30 seconds. To move forward can mean taking many steps back. And then sometimes, a higher power steps in and life's circumstances nudge you to visualize the world you want, and to face the fear that you'll be leaping into new nothingness, charging full-speed ahead toward the future.

Chris never said for certain why he wouldn't go with me to Los Angeles. I'm not sure if he really knew either. Maybe he was scared of my drive for a career, afraid of where that put him in my priorities. And my priorities *were* changing—the relationship that once kept me safe, comfortable, and away from my own intense scrutiny was now a place that I dreaded being in, a place that felt stifling and limited.

The sound of two people growing apart is the slow breaking down of old ideas and beliefs. Chris and I were so exhausted from fighting the change that was taking place between us that the last few months of our relationship were spent in this quiet surrender. I moved out one day while he was at work. It destroyed him, but I wasn't equipped with a better way to do it at the time. I knew that if I looked into his tear-filled eyes, I wouldn't have the courage to leave him or the life we had. Yet something was pulling me away—a greater vision, a deeper calling, and dire responsibility.

The A.C.T. OUT Ensemble still exists today, carrying the message of social issues to young people in Indianapolis, as does the Youth and the Arts summer program, which is now in its seventh year. I planted seeds that will continue to grow and change with the seasons and students they affect. And Chris and I speak occasionally these days. We were both so deep in the muck of our learning that we're still untangling the pain and love we shared. I know that we'll always hold a special place in our hearts and souls for each other.

I moved to Los Angeles with the idea of taking my unique brand of theatrics and dialogue into a televised format. I'm in the process of living those stories now, and will perhaps get a chance to write them down in another book one day. But one thing was and has always been clear to me: *Like me, people are hungry.* We're all starving for loving attention, connection, understanding, and healing. All people, all sizes, all colors, and all classes—all speak the same language, move through the same experience, and long to be satiated by the same human desires. In my young life, that's one thing I know to be true.

That's why I have to tell these stories—and I have to tell *my* story—for all of the voracious souls out there who long to be filled up, and for the very hungry girl who is now becoming a full woman.

✳ ✳ ✳

part II

BINGEING ON LIFE

Stories from the Road

chapter 8

Body Loathing, Body Love

During the six years from 1995 to 2001, I spent my days on the road visiting more than 200 cities and working with 300,000-plus audience members nationwide. I marched my theatrical troupe in and out of small towns, large cities, Ivy League colleges, urban universities, private academies, public schools, Fortune 500 companies, and churches and synagogues.

In the process of booking a gig, I'd learn an incredible amount about the lives of the people who were hiring us. I called them our "sponsors," for lack of a better word. Sometimes the A.C.T. OUT Ensemble lived with these sponsors, staying in their homes and driving in their cars while they toted us from gig to gig. My life has led me into the hearts and homes of people who were just like me so that we could all be given a chance to heal.

The work we did had a way of eating through race, class, and gender lines, and always presented a lesson of some sort. No matter how bored or tired we were of a subject matter—and doing the same kinds of shows for years *will* make you bored and tired—the reasons why we were doing this were always revealed. At the time, I had the foresight to record my experiences on the road through my journal writing—and I've scribbled, spewed, and soared my way through more than 80 journals. The next few chapters include some of my favorite "road stories."

The Mickey Mouse Socks

"Weight. Feelings. Lonely. Hide. Secret. Ugly. Pain. Deny. Pressure. Calorie. Lonely. Hide. Scared. Disgust. Fat. Mirror. Die. Binge. Bones. Hate. Pain. Control. Help. Hope."

I'd written this barrage of words to set the tone and energy of the piece, and they shot out like darts from the mouths of the actors positioned in a triangle onstage. Like a Greek chorus, the actors stood with their eyes focused straight ahead—they were uniform and universal characters painting the air with the language that most men and women use when they talk about eating disorders and body image. And as they finished their round of words, they scurried behind the backdrop and got ready for their next scene.

As I mentioned before, I began piecing together *Body Loathing, Body Love* while in college, as I was unraveling my own pain from my eating disorder. At first, the show only reflected my personal experience, but then it grew to include the voices and stories of others. I continued to experiment with new ideas and scenes over the years, expanding the play to include the issues of men, parents, and sexuality. Today was the first day we were performing this new-and-improved version on tour, at a college in Illinois. We'd been commissioned by the student health center and the athletics program, so we'd spend two days on this brick-and-brown campus showcasing our work to about 300 students.

I took this opportunity to peek at the audience. I watched them cling to each other—and to the notion that this program was most likely going to suck because most programs that schools bring in for "educational" reasons *do* suck—they're pedantic, condescending, and boring. And for most of these students, their attendance on this night was mandatory. Who wanted to address serious topics with a hostile, have-to-be-there audience? After all, it was Thursday at 8:00 P.M.—wasn't *Friends* on or something? It was often an uphill battle to get our message across.

I stood quietly and gazed at the audience while they sat and chatted, ignoring the slides flickering onstage carrying images from fashion magazines and juxtaposed with real art from Chagall, Rubens, and Picasso. Then I closed my eyes and listened. I could intuitively feel the energy by listening to the vibration of their voices, which told me their moods, and if I listened closely, I could also hear their expectations: "God, I don't want to be here," or "My sister's been bulimic for six years."

Observing the audience like this helped me remember why we were here. We were giving them the gift of truth and the opportunity to think. Even though they were forced to be there tonight, I was determined to make it a pleasurable experience.

Back onstage, the show was ready to begin. One of our youngest members, Abby, walked out, placed a stool in its proper position, and began a monologue with nothing else but a fade-in from the music and lights to set the scene: "Did you ever really see me, Dad? What do I have to do to make you proud? Did you ever realize that I need you? I need to hear your words and feel your touch. I lied and said I was full and went to bed early to the rhythm of a thousand sit-ups. I lied and said I was full when all of my food was really in a napkin on my lap. I will just sit in this hole until it becomes my grave. Will you notice me then, Dad? Will you notice me then?"

Pure silence greeted the room. Abby made this piece work because of her eyes—she could cry on cue, and as her emotion surged within her, her big blue eyes brimmed with tears that everyone could see, even from 50 feet away.

I wrote this monologue based on a photograph that a young woman had shown me after a show. It was a Polaroid from the '70s, and it portrayed this girl as a beautiful towhead around the age of five. In the photo, she was sitting at a piano and looking up at a crossed pair of arms that belonged to her father. No face was shown—this was just a snapshot of folded arms and body language

111

that said, "What now?" In the piece, I gave a voice to that little girl. She had such a yearning in her eyes, a desire to be noticed and to feel special.

The girl who showed me the photo said that she'd spent her entire adolescence starving for her father's attention. Her mother had died at an early age, so he was left to raise two girls. As she told me, "He didn't know how to be emotional." So she hid her food in bags and napkins and tried to whittle down her figure so he'd notice and say or do *something*. But he never did. And when I met the inspiration for this piece after a show in Indianapolis, she'd been in and out of hospitals for three years . . . and she was only 20.

The actors continued on, turning in an impressive show that night. Next it was time for our audience-feedback session, which always took some time to get started. I asked for some "brave souls" out there who wished to begin the dialogue. Eventually, someone raised their hand, and we got to talking about warning signs and how to help our friends. No one had commented on Abby's monologue yet, but I knew from experience that it would take a while— girls speaking about their disappointment with their daddies packs a big punch.

A young woman finally stood up in the back of the room, wearing what appeared to be a soccer or field-hockey uniform. She was still sweaty from an early evening practice, even though it was hours later. Her hair was held in a loose ponytail pointing out through the back of her baseball cap. She looked tough, but I noticed that she had on Mickey Mouse socks with her tennis shoes. How tough could she be?

"Why do we have to sit through this shit tonight?"

Her words stung me before I realized what she'd even said. "What?" I asked, absolutely believing that I'd heard her incorrectly.

"Why the hell do I have to sit here and listen to you guys go on and on about some absent dad and some anorexic chick? What does that teach us? Who cares? Everyone's parents are fucked up. I really think this whole play thing is stupid and pointless."

Ouch. Could she have been any more direct? As if in some choreographed stage movement, my actors all turned to look at me for a response. And the rest of the audience was in shock. I cleared my throat and said, "I appreciate your feedback, and I'm sorry if you didn't find this relevant—"

"God, quit being so nice!" she screamed, cutting me off. "And what does the title mean anyway? *Body Loathing, Body Love*—are we supposed to walk out of here *loving our bodies?*" She said this last sentence in a mocking tone reminiscent of Stuart Smalley on *Saturday Night Live.*

Oh my God, I thought. *She's mocking me! How do I turn this around? I'm here to do a show on body image, and a girl wearing Mickey Mouse socks is heckling me. How did this happen?*

She continued to rattle on with her list of complaints regarding the idiotic nature of my program, when I sort of snapped. "Listen," I said, "I completely respect that you may not like the play or understand the need to have this program, but I will not let you disrespect me or the performers just because someone has clearly disrespected you in the past." The words just flew out of my mouth. I was defensive and scared and wasn't used to being challenged about the message of my work.

She stood fuming at me for a second and then said something under her breath as she picked up her backpack and walked out of the auditorium. Two of her friends followed suit. The rest of the audience just sat there in shock. There were no teachers or coaches to intervene or apologize. When a program like this is presented, it's usually mandatory for the students to attend—however, it's highly unlikely that you'd ever find a teacher or coach giving up their free evenings to come sit in.

I turned back to the audience and somehow managed to make a lesson out of Mickey Mouse Girl's outburst by explaining that sometimes people get all riled up with feelings and emotion—which I described as "energy-in-motion"—and that sometimes we release this emotion in all sorts of ways, some appropriate, some not.

A blonde woman from the back of the room raised her hand and said, "I think you guys did a great job. That dad in the monologue is just like my dad. He wasn't very emotional, either. He used to ignore my brother and me because he didn't know how to relate to us. Now my brother's in jail—probably because he didn't feel loved."

I was grateful for her sharing, yet I had to figure out some way to make her point relevant to the evening's message. This happened sometimes—it became a healing free-for-all when the gates were opened, and I never knew what we were going to get.

There was a counselor there that evening because I always made sure that we tapped in to the local resources in case some serious things got stirred up. I felt as if I needed a therapist myself that night, after navigating through the emotional mess of a follow-up session. It was really difficult not to take everything personally and feel like I'd failed somehow. Even though by the end of the night we had 15 women lined up to share their stories and offer me their heartfelt thanks, I was still focusing on the one who got away. I replayed that moment in my head for months. When I finally received our evaluations from the school, I searched for a comment from her—anything to continue our interaction. I was curious about who she was and even would have welcomed more challenging words from her. But there was nothing. I didn't even know her name. I just carried that image of her Mickey Mouse socks exiting the room. And I wondered just how much of her life she saw up on the stage that night.

POWs

The Denver high school where we were scheduled to perform *Body Loathing, Body Love* was giving a facelift to the entire southern part of the school, which included the gymnasium, the library, and the auditorium. This meant that we were to perform our play about eating disorders in the cafeteria. The irony was lost on the principal, who showed us to our space and warned us that the refrigerators would make buzzing sounds every 20 minutes or so—but we were to "ignore it the best you can."

Today was going to be a marathon day for our cast, with three sessions of the same show back to back with a brief break for lunch in between. And the only opportunity for light in this cafeteria came in the form of the bright fluorescent lights. Yet by the second show we were in our groove, and the actors completely forgot that they were emoting their way through the same space that would soon serve Beef Surprise for lunch. The audience was completely enraptured with the scenes, especially one that depicts an older brother who discovers that his younger sister has been eating all the food in the house:

> *Brother:* I tried to cover for you and tell Mom that it was me and my friends who ate all the groceries, but we both know it was you, Kelly. Why?
>
> *Sister:* You wouldn't understand . . .
>
> *Brother:* Try me!
>
> *Sister:* Why should I? Don't you think I hear you and your friends talk about girls' bodies and how "fine" they are or how they're pigs and should work out a little?
>
> *Brother:* Kelly, we don't mean—
>
> *Sister* (interrupting): Well, how am I supposed to tell you that I feel like a pig, an out-of-control pig? This creature who can't control herself or anything around her . . . a big, fat, ugly—
>
> *Brother:* You're not fat, Kelly, and you're not ugly.
>
> *Sister:* Those are words, just words. Don't you understand? I'm numb to you and to the whole world. . . .

Both women *and* men could relate to this issue—whether they were brothers or boyfriends, the men in the audience understood what it was like to repeatedly tell a girl she wasn't fat, only to have her not believe it. The guys were frustrated and pissed off by this. After the show, a few of them spoke candidly about similar conversations they'd had with the women in their lives. They couldn't get past the fact that this issue had nothing to do with food or weight and searched in vain for the reason why innocent and beautiful beings like their sisters or girlfriends could feel so bleak and insecure about themselves.

I explained that it wasn't an argument or point to be understood logically. I knew it was good for the women in the room to hear this and see that guys weren't really the insensitive beasts they're often painted as. The relationship women have with our bodies is fodder for humor and constant mystery for men: They're used to us hating our bodies, and we're used to them wanting our bodies. Rarely do the two sides meet and agree.

By the end of the third show, we'd grown quite fond of our impromptu performance space. The buzzing refrigerator had joined our ensemble nicely and seemed to cooperate with our timing and tempo. For this last show, we'd also inherited a group of young men who all seemed to be in a uniform of sorts. Each of them wore gray sweat suits and sat collapsed against the last row of risers. There were about six of them, and they all looked so familiar, like the brothers of many girls I'd known over the years. Yet they also carried with them an energy that warned me if I was going to be heckled that day, it would be from this group. I was surprised to find them silent during the entire presentation, and even more surprised to see that when it came time to dialogue, the boy in the center of the group spoke first.

He asked me if I'd ever heard of "POW days," and I said that I hadn't.

"Well, that's when the wrestling team is trying to make weight for a match," he explained. "So we all wear these sweat suits with garbage bags underneath and do whatever we can to drop that last amount of weight before weigh-ins. We spit constantly to get the water out of our bodies, and we run around in between classes to build up a sweat. Our teachers know this, so they let us do jumping jacks in the back of the room. Or if some of us get sleepy because we haven't eaten or slept in days, they let us take naps."

No one in the audience seemed to be surprised by any of this.

"What does POW stand for?" I asked.

"'Prisoner of war,'" he answered. "They call us that because of the dark circles under our eyes and our gaunt cheeks. For the weeks leading up to weigh-ins and the wrestling meet, we're considered prisoners of war."

The boy sitting next to him asked, "We want to know if you think this is wrong. Should the school be supporting this? My mom thinks I have an eating disorder. What do *you* think?"

Before I had a chance to respond, the audience members started to offer their opinions right away, and the conversation evolved into a debate about the extreme things many of us subject ourselves to in the name of winning. Someone also pointed out that this school had the best record in the district when it came to wrestling, and it was considered an honor to be on the team.

As I listened to these kids, it seemed that this was a debate that the school commonly heard, but nothing new was ever instituted to teach these young men how to bounce back in the off-season. It was clearly an issue that polarized everyone.

At about two minutes before the bell was scheduled to ring, another member of the team raised his hand. "I know this sounds gross," he blurted out, "but I throw up everything I eat now. At first I did it to make weight, then I started doing it when I was stressed before tests. But now I'm doing it almost all-year round, even in the off-season. I just can't stop."

"You have bulimia!" a young woman exclaimed.

"No, I don't!" he retorted. "Bulimia is a *girl's* issue."

This drew a few laughs, but it blew me away. These wrestlers, the "golden children" at this school, were legitimately questioning whether or not they were over the edge in their quest for the perfect weight. I explained that since eating disorders were about emotions and experiences, it made sense that they could affect each gender the same way because we all experience the same feelings.

The boy in question stayed after the bell rang and sat with me while the rest of the cast broke down our set. He confessed that he was getting sores in the back of his throat that he thought were caused by the acid from when he threw up. He said that some days he couldn't stop thinking about what he was going to eat and how he was going to get rid of it.

Here was a strong 17-year-old boy who was hurting just as much as any girl in the same situation would be. He felt out of control and afraid of what this "little trick" was doing to his body.

117

A few of his female friends stuck around to walk with him back to class, and I could tell that they were proud of him for speaking up.

As the group headed out of the cafeteria, one of the girls pulled me aside. "It was a really good thing that you got the boys talking today," she said. "They needed it. They need help, too. Sometimes they're worse than the girls. But we don't pay attention to it because they're boys."

After that experience, I spent more time focusing on and including men in my programs, not just as witnesses but also as participants. I wanted to give those POWs a voice.

It turned out that the cafeteria space had served us well—candid dialogue, rigorous honesty, and stereotype-busting seemed to be what was on the menu for that day.

✳ ✳ ✳

chapter 9

The Holiday Sweater Club and Bathroom Bonding

As I've traveled across the country, the preoccupation with body size and shape has been the most prevalent concern I've seen in young women. This topic vacillates between the extremes of anorexia, bulimia, and compulsive overeating to the more general and seemingly benign concerns of dieting, nutrition, and staying in shape. Women bond over their body hatred, and sometimes to be a girl in this world means that we have to engage in constant analysis of our worth based on whatever diet plan we're on. No matter what city I've been in, I've heard the same story: Women know that their fellow sisters are hurting and they want it to stop— but not many know how to help.

The Holiday Sweater Club

Soon after I moved to Indianapolis, I received an invitation to a tea at a woman named Camille Bronston's house. I'd never been to a tea before, nor did I have any idea that Camille's house would be located in the city's wealthiest neighborhood. Her house looked like a hotel—it stretched around the corner to take over an adjacent property where the Bronstons had built a tennis court, a swimming pool, and a private clubhouse. It was actually Mr. Bronston's idea for the clubhouse, but his ex-wife and children used it now, years after a divorce that had made the papers and sparked many juicy rumors of infidelity, spousal abuse, and mental breakdowns.

The tea was scheduled right before Christmas, and the leaves had fallen from the trees and landed in a perfect design around the manicured lawn and pebbled path leading up to the front door. When I pulled my Geo Prism up the steep hill to the house, I felt instantly inferior next to the SUVs, Jaguars, and BMWs that dotted the driveway.

I didn't know the proper attire for a tea, so I wore my usual artistic wardrobe choice: black. A 45-year-old woman named Hillary Watson, who probably had never owned anything black in her entire life, met me at the door. She still wore a ribbon in her ponytail, and she sported a reindeer sweater, the kind where Rudolph has a red cotton ball as his nose. Judging by the extensive amount of rhinestones and gems glued on to make up the twinkling sky and the sparkling candy canes, I'm sure the sweater had cost as much as my entire outfit had.

Camille Bronston was brewing a tea that smelled like apples and cinnamon, and she served it with light, buttery cookies and perfect stirring spoons. She also wore a holiday-themed sweater—hers boasted a giant snowflake in bright red, green, and silver hues. In her ears dangled little snowmen, and on her finger was the remnant of her marriage: a giant diamond ring that sparkled as much as Hillary's sweater.

Tea was held in the living room, where family photos hogged the mantlepiece and fought for space with early Christmas cards. I felt as if I'd stepped onto the set for some cooking and lifestyle television show. Everything was color coordinated and very feminine—in my black ensemble I was a dark cloud amidst the yellows, corals, pinks, and baby blues around me. I was so out of place and nervous . . . and I couldn't figure out why I'd been summoned here. This gathering of the "holiday sweater club" (as I would later call them) was made up of some of the wealthiest women in the community. Some of their husbands owned sports teams, others were presidents of banks. In the end, though, they shared a common bond of pain and motherly devotion: Their daughters needed help.

Hillary was the reason Camille had organized this tea and rallied the other mothers to get involved. Hillary told me that her daughter, Ashley, had managed to whittle down her 5'10" frame to 98 pounds, and she'd been in and out of hospitals all year long. This once-vibrant valedictorian of her class and championship swimmer was now a shadow of her former self. These days, Ashley was layered in a deep depression that found her hiding in the house wearing weeks-old pajamas. Hillary wasn't sure what had started her child's descent into anorexia. By all accounts, Ashley had what everyone wanted—including a thin body that had once elicited admiring stares, and the envy of her friends and family. Then things started to get grotesquely out of order—Ashley's ribs showed through her sweater, and her hair began to fall out. Through her tears, Hillary said, "My daughter is dying, Jessica. My husband and I have spent thousands of dollars on doctors and therapists, but we don't know what else to do."

Not every mother who was at the house that day had a child who was struggling with an eating disorder, but all of the girls went to the same elite private school and, consequently, were affected by this issue in one way or another. The mothers claimed that the school was witnessing an "epidemic" of young women with eating disorders. I knew that these girls fit the stereotype: white, wealthy, beautiful, and driven. But as I worked with them, I discovered they were so much more than that.

"We brought you here because we want you to write a play with our girls and show it to their school," Hillary continued. "We came to see your show last year, and it seemed to be the only thing the girls responded to. Will you help them?"

Of course I said yes.

Many of these girls were already into drama and performance. And the school's principal was completely behind our
endeavor, saying that he'd make sure the entire school came to see
our play. The girls and I met a few times a week for four months,
preparing original material based on their lives and experiences,
yet Ashley was so sick that she could barely even make it to
rehearsals. When I finally did get to spend time with her, I discovered that a cousin had raped Ashley when she was nine years
old, and the molestation had continued into her early teens, which
was right around the time her eating disorder had begun. Ashley
didn't know how to tell her mother, so she gave me permission to
share her story with the group, and we wrote a scene about it. This
way, the message could get out there. We all understood that we
were on a consciousness-raising mission so not one more girl
from their school would have to go through this and feel alone.

As I got to know the girls, I got to know their mothers as
well—they were strong, fiercely independent, yet traditional
women who were all dedicated to making sure that their daughters had a fighting chance at a future. If you peeled away their privilege, you'd find scared, confused parents blaming themselves
and willing to throw money at a problem that couldn't be bought.
These women became part of my family while I lived in Indianapolis. Together with their daughters, we helped their school
open up a dialogue on this topic that continues even to this day.

The first performance of our play was additionally charged by
the appearance of Ashley, who sat in the front row bundled in two
sweaters, a jacket, and a scarf. In the end, it wasn't just women up
there, but some men, too—friends of Ashley's who had volun-
teered to add their voices to the piece. The students ended up giving this cast a standing ovation, which doubled as a welcome-back
hug for Ashley.

To celebrate, the moms threw a party back at Camille's house,
and we sat in the same living room where we began. To say thank
you, Hillary and Ashley had bought me a gift. When I opened the
box, I found a Santa Claus sweatshirt, which was odd because it
was now April. But I knew what it meant. "We have to start you

off slowly, you know—you have to build your way up to be a member of the holiday sweater club," Hillary told me with a wink.

Someone had told on me. And I didn't mind. I loved seeing Hillary and her daughter smile.

"Be More of You"

Once during a trip that took my group across three states in six hours, I was in the bathroom of a Greek restaurant that the A.C.T. OUT Ensemble had stopped at for dinner when I saw this woman destroying herself in the mirror. Tears trickled down her face as she kept pulling on her blouse, silently begging it to cover her stomach. She seemed oblivious to the other women moving in and out of the stalls, but occasionally she'd call out to a woman passing by, "Do I look fat in this?" When she tried to reel others into her pain, they shooed past her like she was a freak. I decided to stay and find out what had caused this woman to lose her inner light.

She turned to me and said, "I look like a fat cow, don't I?"

How does one respond to such insanity, especially when staring into the face of such a flawlessly bronzed beauty? I couldn't place her accent, but it sounded as if she was from somewhere in South America. The lilt to her words was familiar from my time growing up in Miami.

She stared at me, waiting for my answer. I said, "I'm not going to answer that question because it's damaging to you." This was a common response I'd trained myself to give when women asked me if they were ugly, fat, or hideous. I continued, "But I can ask what has you in such pain."

She looked at me as though *I* were insane. She took off her shades so that I could see her almond-shaped eyes shining directly back at me. "My boyfriend told me that he slept with my friend last night. He told me this right before he dropped me off here for work. He said that I was fat and that she was more his style." The more she spoke, the more the tears jumped from her eyes and ran across her face, landing on the corner of her white linen top. "So tell me—I'm a fat cow, aren't I?"

I knew something else was going on and that the assault on her self-esteem didn't just begin when this guy dumped her. So I asked her how she felt about her looks.

"I've always hated them," she admitted, "because I'm Latina, and the women in my family have big butts and bellies. And I've always wanted to be skinny and blonde. I'm everything I don't want to be—dark, round, ethnic-looking—when all I really want to do is blend in and have blue eyes and be tall and thin."

Once again, I found myself bonding with a fellow female in a bathroom. I confided to this girl that I, too, had wanted to look like a Barbie doll when I was a little girl. I told her how I'd go to sleep every night and pray that I'd wake up six feet tall and blonde. It never happened—I always awoke looking the same way I had the night before.

She seemed to find solace in my confession.

Then I told her about the work I did and how I saw thousands of women a month who look so brilliantly unique that it made me smile with delight. But these women don't see their gifts—they're too busy chasing a dream created by somebody else. I've seen Asian women come up to me after they've had surgery to have the shape of their eyes emulate the American ideal, sometimes bringing pictures of Britney Spears or Pamela Anderson in to the cosmetic surgeon to use as a comparison. One Korean girl, Kim, told me about the three operations she'd endured so she could have a nose and chin like white girls. The effect of those surgeries had left her scars she was ashamed of—she was wearing her self-hatred on her face for all to see.

I've also held the hands of African-American women from Haiti and the Caribbean who saved up thousands of dollars to undergo liposuction in their thighs and butt, trying to escape a cultural and familial legacy that had been passed down. The inner demons these women battle only reflect an increasing trend in non-white women to develop distorted body image and eating disorders. Our refusal to look at *all* women as beautiful and to honor true diversity in our standards of physical acceptance has forced so many of my sisters to turn on themselves and hate exactly what makes them delicious.

"We don't all drive the same cars," I told this young woman. "We don't eat the same food or wear the same clothes—so why are we determined to look exactly like each other?"

She didn't answer, but I noticed that her crying was subsiding. Next we attempted to figure out why we were so hell-bent on hating our figures or our faces. Where does the hate get us? Further and further away from our true being—miles away from our potential, vision, and sense of self. Now here I was, the former Barbie-worshiping body loather saying that we can't ignore our heritage, the multicultural impact on our dress, entertainment, and speech. Wanting to normalize into an image that's falsely created by the media only buries us deeper in a grave of self-hatred.

I was in a zone. I spoke in eloquent language that flowed from my lips, guided by a much higher source. I was on my way to another performance (this time in Phoenix, Arizona), but I was getting invaluable reinforcement now in this rest room. By the time my diatribe had died down, my new friend's eyes reflected a feeling of relief and peace. "What happened to you today with your boyfriend was terrible," I said. "But it had nothing to do with your weight, your appearance, or your beauty. It has nothing to do with your being Latina or anything like that. You're feeling sad and betrayed, and rightfully so. But you can also choose not to take it out on your body. It doesn't mean you have to change or blend—it means you should stick out *more*. Be more of you."

She pulled her shades back over her almond eyes and straightened out her white linen shirt, allowing it to fall where it wanted to. She applied a fresh coat of lip gloss and wiped the last tear from her cheek. She thanked me—not with words, but with her posture and the glimmer of confidence I saw as she walked past me to go to work. In that moment, she remembered who she was. And I saw what could happen when two women forget to feel fat and decide to feel powerful.

✳ ✳ ✳

chapter 10

The Morning After
and the Untouchables

Just about the toughest subject matter to talk to young people about is rape and sexual assault. People still seem to want to believe that the stereotype of a rapist is the masked man jumping out from behind the bushes, even when they know that teachers, fathers, brothers, counselors, friends, and the clergy rape. And although they may have heard that rape isn't about sex but about power, rarely have they learned how to establish sexual boundaries, understand the reasons behind promiscuity, develop healthy sexual self-esteem, and navigate with self-respect in a highly sexualized world.

The subjects of rape and sexual assault are often married to the topics of alcohol and drug use. Unfortunately, the "Just Say No" '80s ruined it for any educational program that sought to teach the difference between moderate and responsible use and abuse of substances. It was always a challenge to engage in these programs with audiences who came either half baked or completely numb to the message. Yet I never grew numb to all of the confessions of rape and sexual abuse I heard while traveling on the road. In the A.C.T.

OUT Ensemble, we tried to speak up for those who couldn't, to make sense of something so powerfully senseless—even though when we came in to do a program on rape and assault, we had our work cut out for us. No one ever wanted to speak up. People who are raped and assaulted carry the stigma of shame with them. Our society doesn't want to entertain the fact that rapes and assaults are still happening to the people we love. But if we don't talk about it, then the misconceptions and misunderstandings grow, creating more space between the pain and the healing.

The Morning After

One day I got a call from a school telling me that they'd had a "roofies outbreak" on campus. Schools who experience great traumas like this and discover the underbelly of student life on campus like to call things "outbreaks" or "epidemics." I was told that over the course of one weekend, four young women claimed to have been raped by multiple perpetrators at a fraternity party. Since assaults and rapes on college campuses usually go unreported, this seemed unbelievable. Yet at four separate times, four different women walked into the school's health center that weekend, believing that they'd been raped. They'd all undergone tests that indicated they were slipped Rohypnol (or "roofies"), the date-rape drug.

I was hired to institute a program that would ease tensions between the Greek community and those students not involved in fraternity or sorority life. The four women who said that they'd been assaulted weren't in a sorority—and since the alleged assaults had all happened at a frat house, it became fodder for the already anti-Greek campus newspapers. They portrayed the fraternity men in question as barbarians and drunken buffoons raping and beating up innocent coeds. Formal charges and a few lawsuits had already been filed, and the campus had become a hotbed of polarized opinion on rape, sexual assault, drinking, Greek life, and proper retribution. My theater company was brought in to paint a picture that, while compelling and thought-provoking, didn't take sides or lay blame.

The best we could hope for on the night of the presentation was that we would give each side a chance to speak and be heard. But to my surprise, the majority of the audience was male. It turns out that they were forced to attend, so it was no wonder that they meandered in 15 minutes late, reeking of hostility, rage, and alcohol. The women who were there sat to one side of the auditorium, clearly feeling the resentment from the all-male part of the room.

This was only the third time we were performing our new show, *The Morning After*. I still don't like that title—it sounds contrite and overused—but it really does get to the crux of what's left behind after a situation like this: not only personal loss and devastation, but also an emotionally charged campus community, increased tension between the sexes, and perpetuated stereotypes. The aftermath of a rape or assault leaves *everyone* with dark spaces in their hearts.

This play was so effective because it asked the audience to really think about a situation in which there had been drinking, flirting, and poor boundaries set. It was up to them as outsiders to see if they could figure out what had really happened—could they glimpse the story behind a rape?

Laura makes her way around the room, awkwardly picking up her things.

Laura: There's just something I want to get off of my chest. Last night . . . I . . .

Steve: I know what you're going to say.

Laura: You do?

Steve: Yeah, and don't worry. It won't ruin our friendship. We got drunk and hooked up—it's not a big deal.

Laura: Steve, last night we were wasted, but I'm not sure I *wanted* to hook up.

Steve (laughs): Laura, what are you saying?

Laura: Last night, you kept coming on to me—
Steve: And you were coming on to me.
Laura: Okay, but it got to that point, and I didn't want it. I even said—
Steve: What are you saying, Laura? Do you regret hooking up with me? Now you're going to pretend that it didn't even happen? That you didn't want to get together?
Laura: I didn't want to be wrestled to the bed, Steve. I'm not a slut.
Steve: And you're no virgin either. I don't need this crap. [He exits.]

The audience laughed with each honest interaction between the characters. They laughed when Steve called Laura a slut. They laughed when Laura cried to her friend in a later scene. The actors and I expected that reaction—we found that with sensitive topics like this, laughter was a way for people to deal with difficult feelings, and it gave the audience a space to breathe. The dialogue afterwards, however, was heated. The actors playing Steve and Laura stayed in character so that the audience could speak to them about what had happened during their fictional night out. We found that with this play, the audience always analyzed what the woman was wearing and what her previous sexual experiences were. On this night, the crowd used the characters in our play to take out some of their frustration and pain. Some of the guys abused "Laura" as if they knew her by calling her names. And some of the women tried to fire back by asking "Steve" if he liked "having sex with girls against their will." The men and women in the audience barely looked at each other as they hurled questions and insults toward the characters onstage. But it was safe this way.

It wasn't as if these kids were insensitive or cruel. Yet these programs were always emotionally draining for my actors, who had to endure role-playing 'til the bitter end. And we didn't get solutions—we got beginnings. We got opportunities. We got openings in consciousness. We got to meet Anna.

Anna had been quietly sitting in the back. After the last person had left the auditorium, she approached me. She said that she'd just come to watch and was grateful that we'd given her a voice.

There was something about Anna that made me want to reach out and touch her. She had a sparkle, which may have come from the dimple on the left side of her cheek that seemed to elicit a warm reaction to her. You couldn't tell by looking at her that she'd been violated six weeks earlier, except for a little scratch that started at her eyebrow and trickled down to the middle of her cheek. It was faint now, but when that wound had been inflicted, Anna had thought that her face had been split open and her brains were falling out—it hurt that bad.

Anna told me that she'd been flirting all night long with a guy known as "Bones." She said that she did want to "hook up" with him—but for her that meant just kissing and some touching above the waist. Anyway, Anna said that she was pretty sure she'd had five drinks that night. She remembered feeling really sick and tired, so Bones and a few of his friends carried her up to his room so she could sleep it off. Anna's memory was hazy after that, but somewhere along the way, she cracked her head open. She thought it happened when she woke up and found that Bones was inside of her. She then noticed that a few of his friends were watching. When she tried to jerk away, she smacked the side of her face on the headboard. Then she passed out again. The doctors said that they found at least three different semen samples in her the next morning. Someone had written the word *slut* in black marker on her rear end. A nurse alerted Anna to this as she was helping her change back into her clothes. They scrubbed it off together.

Anna told me that as she watched our program, her rosary beads pierced into her skin as the thoughts of what had happened to her pierced her mind and caused her to feel so much guilt and destruction that she wanted to throw up. She carried her grandmother's pearl-and-blood-red beads with her ever since she told her mother about the party. Her mother said she'd go to church to help purge Anna's sins. Anna couldn't even hug her mother because they were speaking on the phone, 400 miles apart. But it wasn't

131

like Anna's mother would hug her anyway. She didn't touch her growing up and believed in tough love and prayer. Lots of prayer. Anna herself was praying that the men who gang-raped her on Saturday night would rot in hell forever.

And Anna wasn't the only one who had gone through this ordeal. There were three other women who had experienced similar assaults over the course of that particular weekend. None of the other women were there that night: One girl had dropped out of school right away, while the others were so traumatized that they couldn't imagine sitting in the same room as their perpetrators. The guys hadn't been kicked out of school yet. In fact, even though there was more than the usual "he said, she said" evidence, they hadn't fully proven in a court of law that these women had been raped. So until then, Anna and the other women had to go to classes and try to remain normal in the most abnormal space they could be in.

I wondered why Anna had chosen to attend our show—the things that had been voiced by the audience were hurtful, ignorant, and so eerily close to home for her. And as I stared at the fading scab that marked a night of terror she didn't remember, I felt horrible that I couldn't do more for her. I couldn't heal her or make it all better—Anna would have to go on to deal and grieve and grow from this experience on her own.

We hugged good-bye, and I said, "I'll pray for you, Anna."

I saw the sparkle rise up inside her as she turned to leave. She said, "No, Jessica, pray for the men who did this. They need it more than I do."

The Untouchables

Coach LeMarx and Coach Harrison took me out to dinner prior to what would be one of the worst experiences of my career. I don't know if they genuinely wanted to treat me to a meal or if they thought that it would help me become more sympathetic to their situation. Jason, their star basketball player, had been kicked off the team for raping and stalking a fellow athlete. It would have been

huge news on any campus, but what made this story so spectac-
ular was that it had taken place in a city within a state that didn't
have a professional basketball team. The locals pumped their
money into this college's team, and by all accounts, the players
were superstars in the community. In fact, that season they went
into the playoffs undefeated. The fear was that without Jason, the
team might falter in the finals. *That* was the fear—not that this young
man might have done something terrible to another student, but
that he might have messed up a chance to win a trophy, thereby
disappointing thousands of fans.

I was speaking solo at a conference on student activism when
representatives from the athletic department of this university
called me up to bring me in for an "emergency session." I didn't
have time to bring my actors with me—not that this department
would have wanted a play anyway. Thanks to school regulations
and an uneasy campus climate, they *had* to provide a program for
the students that addressed what was going on with their star
player. The coaches had heard from other schools that I worked well
under this sort of dire pressure, so they hired me.

Over Italian food, they told me what they were looking for in
this program. "We don't want you to blame Jason or make the students feel any worse about what's happened than they already do,"
said Coach Donald LeMarx. He looked as though he would have
been in the popular crowd in any high school: He was tanned and
toned, and his golden-blond hair was just starting to turn gray. Yet
he made me feel unsafe. I just didn't believe him when he spoke,
even when he said, "I'm a sensitive man—I have three beautiful
little daughters, and I would never want to see them hurt. But I just
don't think that Jason did what that Maria says he did. He may have
harassed her a bit, but she also admits to leading him on."

"We're not saying Maria's lying," Coach Harrison quickly clar-
ified. She was obviously there to be the gender-correct buffer in
the whole situation. She worked in the department as a career
counselor to the athletes and sometimes filled in for the swimming
and diving coach. Neither one of these people knew the victim
directly, but both had been instrumental in recruiting Jason to the

campus three years before—in fact, Mary Ellen Harrison knew Jason's aunt from church and had watched him rise to stardom in high school. It was clear that this kid was a winner—one who was enjoying a full ride to college.

"We all know that Jason can get into some trouble, but right now it's getting blown out of proportion, and our athletes are suffering," Coach LeMarx added.

The "trouble" that Jason had gotten into included bringing a gun to a party. He'd also gotten a DUI his freshman year and was arrested once for fighting in a bar. Those charges were dropped— and people forgot all about it when he scored a three-point shot, just like Reggie Miller, in the final seconds of a playoff game that same year.

I gleaned some information about the victim. Maria had met Jason during her first week of classes. He was a superstar basketball player who was black, and she was a freshman gymnast who was white. He was advanced sexually and had a well-known temper, while she was a shy virgin. How they hooked up in the first place was a mystery to most, but their dating experience wasn't long-lived. She soon met another gymnast and broke up with Jason. Rumor had it that Jason then started calling her all the time, threatening to hurt her new boyfriend. He'd also throw rocks at her window while she studied or page her so often that she had to change numbers twice.

One night, Maria found herself at a party without her new guy and got pretty buzzed. Jason showed up, and they had some words—actually, lots of words that everyone overheard. Witnesses said he called her "psycho" and actually accused her of stalking *him*. She ran out of the house crying and attempted to get in her car, even though she was too drunk to drive. Jason came after her and apologized. He offered to drive her home, and for some reason that Maria will regret forever, she let him.

Once inside her dorm room, Jason started ripping off Maria's shirt. And as he peeled off her pants, he smacked her face. She said that she didn't want to be hit again so she just lay there and let him have his way with her. She cried the whole time. Maria's roommate walked in on them and assumed it was consensual. She even told the other women on the floor that Jason and Maria were hooking up and that she was cheating on her new boyfriend.

Someone told Maria's boyfriend what had happened, so he broke up with her. And she still kept what Jason had put her through a secret. Jason slashed Maria's tires and had something to do with her gym bag getting stolen from the locker room at school—her stuff was found scattered across the lawn right next to her dorm. Maria had finally had enough, so she called the police. They went to Jason's house and warned him that there would be a restraining order against him in the morning and that he was not to bother Maria again. Later that night, Jason, who hates to lose, showed up at Maria's dorm room brandishing a gun. This time, her roommate called the police. Instead of just filing stalking and harassment charges, Maria decided to finally press charges for rape.

✸

I walked with the coaches up the steps to the gymnasium, which had been turned into an auditorium by corralling 400 chairs into wavy rows that stretched to the back of the room. They'd set up a small podium for me in the middle of the makeshift stage. I'd asked for a portable microphone so that I could move in and out of the large crowd, but they didn't provide one. Instead, the microphone I was to use was attached to the podium and allowed me only six feet or so of movement.

The podium was set up so high that it made me feel incredibly distant and disconnected, and the large space onstage was lonely and daunting. Everything about the setup of the equipment and the room itself told me this was going to be a rough experience.

Slowly the kids started to trickle in—body after body clothed in cotton, spandex, or sweats—and they were instructed to sit in sections by teams. A head coach and an assistant coach represented each team. By the time all 400 student athletes had arrived, the air was polluted with indifference, incessant complaining, and occasional loud hoots and hollers. One of the members of the track team was chosen to introduce me. As she began to read my bio, I watched as all of the coaches and assistants filed out of the room. I panicked and turned to Coach LeMarx, who was standing next to me. "Where are they going?" I asked. "Oh, it isn't mandatory for coaches to be here tonight, only students," he replied, not sensing at all that this was a bad thing. I was left with two coaches and 400 angry athletes.

I didn't even make it halfway through my presentation before the heckling began. The guys on the basketball team commented on my breasts, someone called me a bitch, and a bunch of the girls giggled—no one was listening. And Coach LeMarx and Coach Harrison did nothing. I tried every trick in the book: I asked for respect, and I gave my impassioned plea that I understood this was a hard thing to sit through but that it was necessary to hear what each other was feeling. They just spoke over me and yelled to each other. And the angrier I got, the more they fed off of it.

I finally stopped talking and just waited, staring at them with a stone face trying to call their bluff. Then I decided to leave my mike and podium and go into the crowd. This got them quiet— momentarily—but I couldn't say one sentence without being challenged. It didn't help that I didn't have a microphone. I was screaming to be heard . . . in so many ways.

Where was their rage coming from? When did they learn that rape was such a big joke? Who taught them that women lied and men were victimized? Did they learn this from bad movies with predictable plotlines? I'd never felt so much hatred directed at my womanhood before. But I felt even more unsafe with the women in the room who let these men act like animals and either laughed it off or were so involved in their own gossip that they didn't even notice what was going on.

This is what happens when administrators and school leaders dump students into a mandatory program and leave—there's no leadership or example for behavior. But ultimately, they just didn't care enough to see what was going on with the students. The department had to fill an hour to make school officials happy, so that's what they did. You could see the coaches counting down the minutes, even as I told the audience every heart-wrenching story I could come up with.

Since I wasn't being given any creative stimulation, I was forced to rely upon audience interaction. And I *did* see a few faces who were with me. I could always spot an assault victim a mile away in a crowd like this: They'd stare straight ahead, wanting to disappear, but letting me know with their eyes that they were with me. That gave me a moment of relief.

I struggled along for about 45 minutes, and then I just couldn't bear to continue. I tried to get these kids to not only open up about what happened but to also understand what it's like to be dealing with the aftermath of a rape or assault. I told them that rape can happen to anyone—even men—and I shared with them the story of a young man whose fiancée had coerced him into having sex with her by verbally taunting and abusing him. "That guy was a pussy!" was what I heard from the crowd.

For some reason, I decided to really open up to them. I don't know why—maybe out of desperation. I talked about how rape is about power and control and that, contrary to popular belief, most women don't lie about it. I tried to make eye contact with the hecklers as I told them how Mark had hit me in college when I went to break up with him. And then I heard a man say, "Someone needs to slap that bitch again and get her to shut up." He was referring to me. I was being assaulted by the room I was brought in to heal.

I stood once more in silence. I stared at the floor, fighting back tears—I was *not* going to let them see me cry. But I couldn't control it. I raised my head, and a tear slid down my cheek. My strength silenced the room enough for me to say, "I have never felt so much disrespect and rage in my entire life. It makes me think that you're *all* guilty and responsible for what happened here. If the way you treated me here tonight as a guest is the way you treat people in your community, then you're creating one sick place to live. You have wasted my time tonight, and I have nothing more to say to you."

They were silent as I walked offstage. Then someone started to applaud and laugh, and I heard the chairs scrape the floor as they rushed to get out. I plopped down on the floor behind a curtain and sobbed—and neither one of the coaches came back to check on me. On this campus, on this night, these athletes were untouchable, protected by ignorance and arrogance.

I hid behind the curtain for a while. I was so embarrassed by what I'd done. I'd never walked out on a show, or even come close to it. And I'd certainly never lost it in front of a crowd. But I was so leveled by the deep disgust and disregard they had for me, the situation, the people involved, and the gravity of what it meant to be raped and assaulted that I couldn't help but take it personally.

✳ ✳ ✳

chapter 11

Missing Michael and 9/9/99

Our society is numb to violence. Yet we consume it, absorb it, and fantasize about it. We purchase it with our money, speak it in our language, and express it in our rage.

When the unreal violence we saw on our TV and movie screens began to spill over into our schools, we all panicked, blaming the availability of guns, the entertainment industry, the media, and peer pressure. Yet we rarely bothered to look in our own backyards. We didn't want to see the way our parents looked at, spoke to, or touched each other. We didn't want to see the beatings that went on in the schoolyards, locker rooms, or bedrooms.

Unfortunately, there just isn't one pat answer as to why there's so much violence in our society. It's a complicated morass of mixed messages and misplaced morals. It isn't someone else's job to stop this violence; it's ours. We have an opportunity every day to live a life free of violent thought, word, and deed. For this, we're all responsible.

Missing Michael

Michael Richardson tried cocaine for the first time during his freshman year of college. He'd grown up in a small farming community on the border of Indiana and Illinois—in fact, his town was so small that there were only 39 people in his graduating class. Michael had a handful of friends and loved good ol' country music. He made grain alcohol with his grandfather but never had the urge to drink it. Yet when Michael got to college, he discovered that he liked to get high with someone from his organic chemistry class. They'd smoke weed together on the weekends and then go get a sandwich and walk through town, laughing at the other drunk and stoned people.

Michael easily blended in on campus. He was an average student who'd entered this Midwestern school determined to be a more successful engineer than his brother. Instead, he turned out to be a loner with a secret. He couldn't explain his sudden descent into sleepless nights and hopeless thoughts. He just started to hate life as soon as he started college. He was depressed and suicidal and hid it from everyone—including his resident advisor, Rich, who frequently checked on the new student to make sure he was acclimating to campus.

Rich noticed that something was different about Michael after a hall meeting one night during the spring semester. Rich thought Michael looked really wound up and angry, as he blew Rich off and left the meeting early to go meet a friend in his room. This was the same friend from organic chemistry—only now they were dabbling in less organic chemicals, such as cocaine and crystal meth. No one would peg these two for druggies: Michael had just started doing coke to stay awake to study for the science tests that gave him such headaches and anxiety.

Michael's older brother, Matthew, had been a brilliant scientist until his body was found floating in a river. He had jumped from a nearby bridge, leaving a note that simply said "Sorry"— no explanation, no signature, nothing. Michael was 16 at the time and vowed to replace Matthew's role in the family by doing everything his brother liked to do, such as going bowling, writing poetry, and studying science—none of which Michael personally cared for. He also followed in his brother's path by struggling with low-grade depression and anxiety. He went on two different kinds of antidepressants, but neither did the trick. Michael was obsessed with thoughts about death, and he intensely buried the rage he felt for living a life unfulfilled and ignored. Michael wrote these feelings down in many practice suicide notes that he kept in a drawer by his bed.

Rich had been an R.A. for three years, and was getting ready to graduate and move to St. Louis to go to nursing school with his fiancée, Marcy. Rich was the nice guy who always did the right thing. Even as an R.A., when his job was to keep order and write up people for illegal partying, no one got mad at him when they were busted. He was just that kind of guy. So when Rich knocked on the door of Michael's room to check on him, he was surprised that he was told to "Go the fuck away."

Michael may have been a quiet loner, but he wasn't a jerk. Rich knew something was wrong and demanded to be let in. When Michael finally opened the door, he was so high that he could barely keep his head up. He puked all over Rich before he could even get in the room.

Michael was put on academic probation right away for having drugs on campus. For some reason, he wasn't prosecuted for having cocaine—some people thought that Rich had pulled a few strings to get Michael a second chance. For a while it seemed as though things had calmed down. The rumors and the stares from people living on Michael's floor stopped circulating, and he soon went back to being ignored. The end of the semester came, and it was time to go home for the summer. Finals were completed, and Michael had managed to fail most of his classes. He took an incomplete in organic chemistry, since he hadn't shown up for class in over a month. Slowly, his rage and desperate thoughts of killing himself grew. The notes in the drawer by his bed doubled. He was living a quiet life of isolated, painful numbness. And by this time, he was fully addicted to drugs. Rich found Michael passed out in the bathroom with cocaine still under his nose—and this time he

141

notified the campus police. Michael was arrested, and his friend from organic chemistry bailed him out. Then his life came crashing down. The administration instructed him to go back to his dorm room and pack up his things, for he wasn't going to be allowed back to school the next year.

No one knows where Michael got the gun—he'd probably had them at home on the farm. He somehow managed to keep a sawed-off shotgun in his closet. Once back in his dorm room, he took out one of the pieces of paper that explained the silent torment he endured and how he was "tired of taking pills just to function." He raged against the world in this note, and most surprisingly, he railed against Rich. Rich was the person Michael wanted to be: comfortable in his skin, well liked, and in love. Michael hated him for it. He wrote of ripping Rich's head off and throwing his body off the same bridge that his brother had leapt from. He blamed Rich for getting him kicked out of school and mercilessly attached all of his hatred to his unsuspecting R.A.—and no one would really ever know why.

Michael packed only one suitcase before he loaded the shotgun. He did one line of coke and took about 20 of his antidepressant pills, and then he took off down the hall to find Rich. Michael didn't hide the shotgun at all—and the sad thing was that the handful of people who passed him in the hall didn't even notice that he had a gun. They didn't pay any attention to Michael until he knocked on Rich's door, pushing it open to reveal Rich and Marcy kissing. Marcy screamed when she saw Michael's gun, and that alerted everyone that Michael could no longer be ignored.

I was in the midst of defending an application for a grant to perform work about drug and alcohol abuse in the same county where Michael was proving my point: that beyond the usual partying, students of all kinds were afflicted and affected by drug use in college. At the time, this grant committee just didn't get it. They didn't believe that their humble small town would ever feel the sting of drugs or violence that the inner city did, so they were in the process of declining my grant proposal. That's when we heard that a student at the university had used a gun to barricade himself in a room with his resident advisor.

The police surrounded the dorm where Michael held Rich hostage and evacuated most of the students—fortunately, it was in the middle of the afternoon, so most of the kids were in class. The news trucks and reporters were out in front getting ready to spin their stories when three shots rang out. Up until that time, the police had tried to reason with Michael through a loudspeaker, begging him to hand over his gun.

It turns out that Michael made Rich read his suicide note out loud to Marcy before he shot Rich in the head. Michael then turned the gun on Marcy, as she hid under Rich's body screaming and crying. Michael fired the next bullet out the window toward the police cars; before they could fire back, he shot himself in the head. No one knew why he didn't kill Marcy.

I was still living with Chris at the time and I raced home to share what was happening with him. He had already heard about it on the news by the time I got there. As we watched TV together, I noticed that the entire community seemed amazed that something like this had happened at their prestigious university. Chris just held me on the couch for hours because I was so freaked out. The next thing I knew, I got a phone call from the grant committee. They had reconsidered my proposal and were granting me the funds to do my program under one condition: I had to create a piece especially for this situation and pre-sent it in three days for the grieving students before they left for the summer. I immediately called my actors and began to prepare.

We put together an abstract movement and monologue show called *Black Octopus.* I chose to create a nontraditional piece so that we could tap in to the emotion of the grief and not logically analyze or explore it with dialogue and realistic scenes. I felt that the students had had too much realism in their lives for the moment.

The lead character was a young loner named Bobby, who used drugs and the escape they offered to run away from a life blurred by mental illness and depression, just as Michael had.

Bobby stands still onstage as the dancers and actors move around him and drape him in a black cloth, covering him from head to toe. The actors echo his words.

Bobby: You don't think this can happen to you?
Chorus: You!
Bobby: I was swimming in a sea of loneliness
and anger.
Chorus: Anger!
Bobby: That's where I met the Black Octopus and it
helped me drown.
Chorus: Drown!

Actors pick up the cloth over Bobby's head and drop suddenly to the floor. Bobby is no longer there. The stage is empty.

When the piece was over, we all sat on the edge of the stage and looked into the audience. They were silent, crying and confused. Their worlds were rocked. I asked for a brave soul to begin the conversation. Someone raised their hand, and so we began the process of trying to heal. . . .

9/9/99

"Columbine will happen here," had been spray-painted on the lockers of this suburban Denver high school. And *"9/9/99 is the day you all will die!"* was the second threat found painted in the boys' bathroom on the first floor of the school. This graffiti was taken so seriously that the FBI had been called in. After all, Columbine High School was only about five miles down the road, and the tragedy that had occurred there was less than six months old.

There were roughly ten school shootings that happened before Columbine that made local and national news: including those in Pearl, Mississippi; Paducah, Kentucky; Jonesboro, Arkansas; and

Springfield, Oregon. The A.C.T. OUT Ensemble had been commissioned by many schools to write a reaction piece to the shootings in order to commence a more in-depth dialogue about school violence and bullying. *Battered Souls* explored the life of a shooter named Jeffrey before he decided to go on a rampage. It attempted to unearth a "why," the word so many of us utter when we first learn of a tragedy. In our show, we began backwards from the first news report of the incident and retraced the steps of Jeffrey's life to show some of the root causes for the alienation, isolation, and bitter resentment that plagued him. We knew we didn't have the answers, but we were once again attempting to open up a space for healing and conversation.

The show opened with a schoolyard scene, physically blocked out in slow motion. We showed kids walking to class, laughing and telling jokes, and making fun of other students, while Jeffrey stood on the side of the stage, reading a poem to the audience. He was in real time while the action behind him painted a slowed-down backdrop of his world.

> *Jeffrey:* Every day you wait for me after school
> And call me fat, ugly, stupid, and slow
> I hate you more than I hate myself
> Someday I will be the star of this show
> At home there is no escape
> No place to run and hide
> The hate is there at home
> The pain lives deep inside
> Did you think I was invisible?
> Did you think I couldn't hurt?
> As you spit on me and pushed me
> As I fell into the dirt . . .

Jeffrey now moves onstage, delivering his poem directly to the actors who still move in slow motion and are oblivious to Jeffrey. They're busy picking on and ridiculing another student. He continues:

I am all alone
No one cares about what I do
All the pain that you cause me
Will come flying back at you
I dream of a way out
A plan to make you pay
When you least expect it
That will be the day
Then I will show you
That I hurt . . .

Gunshots ring out, bringing the entire scene from slow motion to chaos. Kids run screaming and scrambling for cover, while Jeffrey stands still in the middle of the stage holding a gun.

Right about the time that Eric Harris and Dylan Klebold entered Columbine High School and started taking the lives of their peers, we were joking around, mocking each other's performance of a play that we'd done more than 30 times in the past several months. That day in rehearsal, the actor playing Jeffrey was goofing off by kissing his schoolyard bullies on the cheek instead of looking at them sourly. And someone had replaced the gun Jeffrey carries in his backpack with a banana, which of course someone did something obscene with later on in the scene. Most of the cast couldn't stop laughing long enough to deliver their lines.

I was having a ball along with them, parodying our work and the seriousness of the subject matter. We were in our fifth year traveling the country, and this particular company was exceptionally close. We had lots of inside jokes, along with the usual bonding stories an artistic company shares. We were especially silly right before we got ready to go out on the road—the gravity of the work we did required us to blow off some steam. I loved playing around with them, and was in the middle of roaring with laughter when our secretary at the theater interrupted us to tell us to turn on the TV.

At the time, the news had confirmed that 12 students and one teacher had died at Columbine High School, and they weren't

146

sure how many others were injured. There in front of us were the images of kids stampeding across the schoolyard, crying, screaming, and running for cover. What we'd just played out onstage moments ago was eerily happening in real life. Our eyes, along with the nations', were glued to the TV set in utter disbelief. It had happened again, and once again we were all uttering that word: *Why?*

Many of my cast members began sobbing, feeling guilty for playing and making light of the situation. I gave them a pep talk before sending them home: "We were just living in the moment, having fun," I said. "Our lightness and irreverence is human, and the work we do is important. You take a lot on when you do this show, and you deserve to blow off steam and play. Please take it easy on yourselves." With that, I cut rehearsal short to go home and watch the news coverage. I was floored by just how much life was imitating our art and our art was imitating life. At this point in my career, the divine irony of timing was not lost on me—I knew that our work and messages showed up where they were needed. And I knew that unintentional miracles had a way of finding those who needed them, just at the right time.

We'd originally been booked to perform *Battered Souls* at a youth and violence conference in Denver and Boulder that fall, but the dates of our appearances were moved up after the events of Columbine made the news. When we arrived at this particular school on, yes, 9/9/99, our bags were searched, our slides and props examined, and we had to go through makeshift metal detectors, which many schools had erected since the Columbine shootings.

School officials were trying to conceal the real tension they were feeling. Many of the young people floating around the halls were transfer students from Columbine—too many of them had already lived through one tragedy and they didn't want to unnecessarily alarm them. I was alarmed, though: We were getting ready to perform in a school under FBI surveillance and encountering death threats. But what made it worse was what happened next.

Susan Reed, the assistant principal, pulled me aside while we were en route to the auditorium to set up for the show. She had sweaty palms when she shook my hand. I wasn't sure whether that was a usual ailment or a symptom of the day's activities. She said, "Listen, Jessica, I know you were prepared to perform your show on school shootings, but I don't think that's a good idea today. I want you to focus more on conflict resolution and anger management. I don't want you to mention Columbine—not at all."

What?! I internally screamed. Even if I were to move past the fact that she told me to can the entire show that we'd brought across the country less than 30 minutes before showtime, I still couldn't believe that she'd just told me to ignore the biggest, pinkest elephant in the room. I was getting ready to face 500 students who had all been intimately involved in the Columbine massacre, and I wasn't suppose to talk about it? How does one address conflict resolution when the most obvious example of that came in the form of semi-automatic guns, pipe bombs, and bloodshed in a high school right next door? Obviously Eric and Dylan had ignored those catchy phrases of "Fight with your words, not your fists" or "Just walk away and count to ten."

Susan Reed left me immediately to go attend to other school business, so I was left to tell my actors that there had been a change in plans. I knew that if I went against Susan's wishes, I could possibly be kicked out of the school and certainly wouldn't be able to pay the actors for their work, so I had to find a halfway point to get across a more realistic message while entertaining her completely skewed beliefs. My actors worked extraordinarily well under pressure, so together we began to craft some improvisational scenes that could take the place of the scripted work we'd prepared.

I looked to my assistant director to create quick characterizations and plotlines that we could leave open-ended for the audience to resolve. This was an old-school theater trick that we used many times to engage the audience into interaction and investment. I called them "explosion scenes": We'd work up a few minutes of a scenario that would halt at the point of conflict, and then I would facilitate an alternate ending with the audience. At least this way I could get the students to hear their own voices today, even if Susan Reed was trying to censor the dialogue. I figured that if we put the power back in the hands of the students by asking them to solve the situations differently, then it might give them a new sense of empowerment, strength, and hope.

The actors were backstage working out their new blocking. I sat on the front of the stage as the audience poured in, wanting to feel them out and a get a sense of who they were, as I usually did with a crowd. They felt like normal high school students to me—you never would have guessed that they lived right next door to a national tragedy. In fact, we'd passed Columbine High School on the way to this school, and it felt as if we were seeing something we'd only read about in books. Columbine became larger-than-life due to all of the media attention it had received—yet when we saw the school with its windows still boarded up and awaiting repairs, and when we saw the front lawn those young people had marched across with their hands on their heads in single file, it seemed like we were really just seeing an abandoned movie set.

Two girls wearing blue backpacks interrupted my ruminations about Columbine. "Are we gonna get to talk about it?" one of them asked me.

"Talk about what?" I inquired.

"Talk about what happened. *No one* will talk about it."

"It's weird," the other girl said. "I mean, they're punishing us if they catch us being mean to people because they think that's what made Eric and Dylan do it. But no one's talking about how it feels."

"How *does* it feel?" I asked.

The first girl turned around and showed me her backpack. Up in the corner by her right shoulder were two tiny holes, and under it a small patch was sewn on. The patch was in the shape of a heart and the initials D.W. were written in the middle of it in blue ink.

"My best friend died at Columbine," she replied. "We were studying in the library. They must have shot at me, too, but it went through my backpack. I keep wearing this backpack to remind me that my best friend died, but I didn't."

My throat was dry and my eyes were watering, as the intense reality of the situation hit me. I had the daunting and blessed task to create a space for healing today—these kids were literally asking for it. In all of my time doing this work, I'd never really felt scared or inadequate. In that moment, I felt both.

The girls stayed with me as people took their seats in the predictable cliques of high school. There was the goth section, the jock section, the geek section, the drama kids section, the preppie section, and way in the back sat a small group of kids with black trench coats. The girls gave me scoop: "Those kids in the trench coats think that what Eric and Dylan did was kind of cool. They're those kids' heroes in a way," one of my new friends explained. "Everyone hates them, and the school is watching them. Our principal thinks that they're the ones who wrote that stuff on the lockers."

I stared in their direction for a minute and did a gut check on myself: Yup, I was still feeling inadequate—and now I was *really* scared. The bell rang, and I saw Susan Reed appear onstage to do my introduction. She not only mispronounced my last name but also threatened the audience with detention if anyone acted out. My whole motivation was to get the students to act out and be involved, and now they were warned that they'd be scolded for doing so. Consequently, I tripped over my words trying to censor myself and delete my honesty and intuition.

About 15 minutes into our show, Susan Reed and a row of teachers exited the auditorium. I was left, as I'd been on many occasions, to fly solo without school support for a subject matter so treacherously important and serious. Our improvisational scenes tanked—the actors could feel my tension, and the audience could certainly see through our underprepared storylines. And when I asked the crowd for input on a scene about picking a fight with a classmate, their autopilot answers were "Kill him, kick his ass, bring a gun to school and shoot him." They used that rote response for everything, trying with all their might to evoke a Jerry Springer-like chanting during the acted-out conflicts.

The kids were completely removed from the situation, emotionally brainwashed and speaking in sound bites. When I changed course and asked them to tell me why we had so much violence in our schools, they bypassed any thoughtful process of answering and went straight to quick-fix answers such as, "There are too many guns available" or "There's too much violence on TV." They'd seen these media-coached clips played out before them on every news channel on television. Many of these kids and their families had become local celebrities based on the national morning shows they'd appeared on. Some even had book deals and movie producers sniffing around to secure rights to their stories. Before me sat the students on the front line of this war between our perceived view of adolescent life and its violent, harsh reality. They were the walking wounded, disconnected souls who, if left as they were, would be doomed to repeat history and perpetuate the cycle of violence. I'd never paid much attention to the politicians who argued over too much violence on TV and in video games because I always thought that life experiences made us violent, not a song lyric or a movie character. But I was seeing the true effect of a steady diet of programs devoid of humanity, love, and unifying messages.

More important, I was seeing firsthand what happens when we suppress uncomfortable dialogue and attack an issue on the surface, never lancing the boil and clearing out its core—when we ignore emotion because it feels dangerously overwhelming and intense; when we don't allow for healing to look messy and feel messy; when we don't have the answers for life's tragedies, yet pretend we do; and when we deny our children and ourselves the right to feel and express anything and everything.

I had to do something. The actors and I were failing miserably at connecting with the audience because we weren't speaking our truth. I jumped up onstage and asked the actors to stop mid-scene. I instructed them to create two obstacle courses using any material they could find backstage, including chairs, tables, books, and theatrical props. While they did this, I went into the audience with my microphone and stood in front of our disconnected students. "Look," I said, "what we're doing clearly isn't working. Okay, it sucks." They laughed. "And I'm sorry," I went on. "We were trying to speak around an issue that we can't ignore." I looked around the room. Since Susan was still gone, I decided to go for it.

"I know you all recently lived through something really horrific. I really have no idea what that feels like. We just watched it on TV—you were there. And I'm so sad, as I'm sure you are. I don't know what to say except that I want to figure out a way for us to treat each other better without sounding like a greeting card." They laughed again. I had it. I had my truth back. "So here's what I want to do. I want to play a game."

They looked stunned. I'd just turned this whole thing around and was now moving from the anger-management lady to the game-show hostess. "I'm going to pick two teams to play this game," I said, while looking out into the audience to select members of my experiment.

I made my choices completely based on outer image and stereotype. On one team I placed a jock, a few drama kids, a couple of geeks, and one goth girl with a black heart painted on her cheek. I tried to pick people who looked as if they'd never communicate with each other. The next team I picked consisted of the same type of kids: all preppies and cheerleaders.

I gave both teams these simple rules:

"You must put yourself in alphabetical order, first name first."

"Your feet can't touch the ground at any time. You must stay on top of these objects."

"And you must do it in silence. You *cannot* speak to each other with your voice."

The audience howled with laughter, convinced that the first team didn't stand a chance, since it was likely that no one even knew each other's names, as all came from such different circles. But what we all saw next reminded me that there are angels out there.

I gave both teams a time limit of two minutes. Almost immediately, the jock, who was the natural leader of the first group, took charge and figured out that the goth girl's name began with an "A" because one of the geeks showed him in sign language. Then the whole team caught on, and not only did they sign out the first letters of their names to each other, but they also started to communicate and work together nonverbally. The jock reached across two geeks and a drama kid to pick up the goth girl and carry her to the front of the obstacle course since their feet couldn't touch the ground. Their teamwork was effortless and beautiful to watch. The audience went back and forth between cheering wildly and sitting in absolute silence, absorbing that these complete opposites had come together so quickly and painlessly to win the exercise. The preppies and cheerleaders, who weren't faced with such a big challenge since most of them knew each other's names, didn't complete the exercise in time. They spent their turn joking around and playing because they were more comfortable with each other.

At the end of the two minutes, team one was the victor by placing each other in alphabetical order: Allison, Andrew, David, Gary, Jeff, Sandra, and Terry.

The audience knew intrinsically what had just happened. A pattern was broken, a taboo was discussed, and a new paradigm was formed. The message was simple and so clear: There's always an opportunity to make a change. And when you just get down to it, you can work together with *anyone* if you're willing and you share the same goal. So I asked the kids to consider making their goal a violence-free existence at school (to the best of their ability) and a kinder, more open social environment. I was well aware that it's a teenage requirement to experience communal angst, and it's practically a rite of passage to feel ostracized, but they certainly didn't need to hurt each other as they went through this time in their lives. I think they got it. It was just a step, a small step toward making a change. Looking back, it seems too simple in relation to what had happened in their community, but in the moment it was exactly what they needed to feel not so alone.

A group of students, including the girls with blue backpacks, stayed after the bell rang to process what had just happened. Allison, the goth girl with the painted face, stayed, too. She told me how she has to eat lunch sitting in the hallway in between the lockers and the front door. She has to see an exit sign and a clear path to the door because she says at Columbine she was trapped in the cafeteria with no way out. To protect herself from the bullets, she piled lunch trays and chairs up around her, but she couldn't escape since the shooters were blocking the doorways. The girls in blue backpacks nodded in agreement.

Jeff, the jock on Allison's team, came by to say thank you. And he added, "You know, I can't even study in the library anymore because I keep expecting someone to come in and start shooting. Our whole lives have changed, and no one really understands."

As the actors and I made our way out of the school that day, we walked through the crowded hallways of students eating lunches together, huddled in familiar cliques that gave them safety, keeping an eye on the door and on each other. And I realized that Jeff was right—I never will understand what it feels like to have a war declared in my own school.

✳ ✳ ✳

chapter 12

Coming Full Circle

When you do work that comes from the heart, you don't really think about it. My adventures on the road happened organically, and I learned a lot simply by showing up and being of service. The stories unfolded, the people spoke up, and in the end, we all moved forward. There were, of course, some great moments that resonated in my being, experiences that taught me a great deal about myself. With this kind of unique work, there's no predetermined path. I had the extraordinary opportunity to pry, peek, and plop right into the lives and journeys of other people. And I realized in the end that I didn't choose the work, *it chose me.* As I agreed to heal and help others along the way, I received lessons of humanity, strength, and fortitude. I knew I wasn't alone doing this work because a higher presence placed gentle victories, rough obstacles, and beautiful people before me as gifts, reminders that I was on the right path.

She Found Me Again

This show was going to be like any other. We were doing *Body Loathing, Body Love* for the entire sorority system at a major university in the Southwest—about 600 women were expected to show up. It was the last stop on our spring break tour, and the last show we'd be doing together as a company. I'd decided to move on and head west to try my hand at television. After Columbine, I was infused with a passion to bring our theater company's message to a larger audience in a more accessible format.

We were all sad, but we didn't show it—instead, we were in rare form, cracking jokes and hugging each other as we set up the stage and props for the very last time. After hundreds of performances to hundreds of thousands of students, we thought we'd seen it all. We were more than a social-issue theater company, we were a traveling soap opera and study in human nature. I'd seen my actors and technicians through addictions, arrests, pregnancies, abortions, divorces, eating disorders, deaths, suicide attempts, car accidents, custody battles, cat fights, romance, adultery, deep friendships, artistic breakthroughs, personal triumphs, and all forms of abuse. These weren't storylines we made up—this was the stuff of our lives, which mimicked and mirrored exactly what we presented to our audiences. We lived in our truth and used it in our art as best we could.

We did our usual preparations, then we huddled together as a group and had a teary final pep talk before the show. It was only fitting that our last show would be the same as our first, and it featured the subject matter that had started this whole movement for me. *Body Loathing, Body Love* was a constantly evolving work in progress—as I grew in my recovery, I rewrote scenes and monologues to reflect new lessons I'd learned. And as more brave souls came forward to share their stories, I'd included their voices as well. This show had become a collective gathering of experience, strength, and hope, mustered from emotional talk and lots of miles on the road. It was by far our most popular and needed show. I'm sure my actors got sick of playing the same bulimic characters, but I never tired of hearing truthful realizations from the people who were at the beginning of their healing cycle.

On this night, the show was flawless, sparkling from the actors' extra energy. A new bit I'd written brought down the house and got us a standing ovation before the play was even finished. It was a spoken-word piece entitled "Who Says," which I'd begun writing when I was in college. It reeked of '60s guerilla theater and beatnik poetry jams, as the actor delivered her words directly to the faces of audience members, climbing on chairs in front of them, sitting beside them, or sometimes even winding up in their laps. Behind the performer, there would be a video or slide presentation showing images of women from all over the world—including paintings and photographs of celebrities and "real" women alike. I wanted the audience to see what different women really looked like.

All modern conventions of the stage were thrown out with this piece that asked the question: *Who says that as women we were to hate, mangle, and destroy our bodies all in an effort to fit in?*

From the audience, the actor speaks:

> Who says
> Who says my soft white belly must be
>   brown and lean
> Who says I should starve
> Who says I should watch my weight
> Who says be pretty
> Be smart
> Be nice
> Who says don't disappoint
> Who says you can't do that
> Who says dress nicely
> Wear makeup
> Be stylish
> Who says deny
> Who says control
> Who says pretend

Who says
Who says look in magazines
Who says change yourself
Who says be the same
Look like me
Look like you
Who says shhhhh
Be quiet
Don't speak
Who says not good enough
Not thin enough
Who says no
Who says no
Who says, who says, who says
Who says I should be anything but what I am
Who says punish myself
Who says eat
Who says work harder
Be better
Always win
Who says don't laugh
Who says be polite
Who says be perfect
Be like me
Be like you
Who says don't get mad
Keep it inside
Who says don't fight back
Don't give up
Let it go
No big deal
Who says, who says, who says
I say
Go to hell

Our final feedback session went off without a hitch. We weren't particularly surprised by any of the commentary—all of the usual

anger, sadness, curiosity, and social issues came out. After we'd perform this show, most of the questions would revolve around how
to help a friend or loved one. People wanted to see the hurting stop.
On this evening, a young woman shared her frustrations about her
anorexic roommate, who was working out incessantly at all hours
of the night, keeping her awake and worried. We explored ways
in which she could speak with her roommate and encourage her
to get help. She was given the number of the student health center. There was no heckling, no breakdowns, no resistance, or
snotty remarks. There were tears, there was laughter, and there were
good spirits. All in all, it was a perfect way to end the night—not
with a bang or whimper or high drama, but with a good, solid show
offering service to emotionally available young women. Then God
kicked in and decided to give me a real send-off.

"Any other questions or comments before we wrap it up?" I
asked the crowd, already thinking about what I needed to pack for
the trip home. Since no one said anything, I said, "Well, I just want
to thank you because this will be our last show. We're closing down
the company after six years and a lot of magical experiences.
Thanks for being such a great last audience."

As the first hands got together to clap and the first butts arose
from the seats, a young woman in the middle of the auditorium
stood up and screamed, "Wait! I have something to say."

The crowd took a minute to wind back down, and then she
asked, "Do you remember me?"

As she came closer, I thought, *Oh God, should I?* She had short
light brown hair and was wearing a matching teal sweater set with
a pair of black dress pants. She looked like a zillion other women
I'd come across over the years. So far, nothing about her seemed
familiar.

"I'm sorry, I don't," I said, hoping that my last night wasn't going
to end in some dramatic confrontation after all.

"I saw you do your first performance of this show at my school
in Illinois about six years ago," she said. "I was pretty mean to you.
I think I even cussed you out." The girls all giggled.

She looked a bit older than the rest of the audience, but I still
couldn't place her face. "I was so angry with you for being there

that night," she continued. "My coach made me come from track practice, and all I wanted to do was go home and binge and purge, and then there you guys were, showing me pieces of my life and I really, *really* hated you for it."

Oh my gosh, it was my first heckler—the girl wearing Mickey Mouse socks.

She turned to the rest of the students in the audience. "I wanted to stand up here and tell you guys what this woman and her company did to change my life. When I saw this play six years ago, I was a freshman in college and about four years into my disease. I was bulimic—throwing up like ten times a day and also abusing laxatives and diet pills. I was even thinking about killing myself. I saw my entire life up there on that stage, and it freaked me out. I couldn't stop thinking about it. I didn't know that anyone else could understand what I was going through."

I felt tingles all up and down my body. The entire room blurred, as I just tried to focus on what she was saying while remaining present to hear her. I was in complete shock that this was unfolding as it was.

She turned back to me and said, "I dropped out of school soon after I saw your play, and I went into treatment for my eating disorder. That's when I discovered that I was bipolar, too. I was in and out of hospitals for two years, but then I finished my degree. I transferred out here last spring to begin graduate school—I'll be getting my master's in counseling with an emphasis in eating disorders so that I can help other people like you helped me."

The tears flowed down my cheeks. I felt raw, exposed, and vulnerable as I stood onstage surrounded by my performers, my words, my work, and the absolute honesty and humanity of a life I only dreamed of living. I let her words in as she continued.

"I thought about you a lot over the years, but I never knew how to get in contact with you. Then one day I passed by a poster for your show on the bulletin board. I about flipped out. I knew I had to come by and see you and say thank you. Oh, by the way—I thought your show got a lot better." The audience laughed again with a sweet release of emotion.

"Always a critic," I shot back with a huge smile on my face. "You really cussed me out back then."

She laughed. "I know. I really hated you for showing me my life. But in the end, you saved it."

For this interchange, we received another standing ovation—and by this point the rest of my company was also sobbing, realizing the power of the situation and the lasting legacy they'd helped to create. We had an unusually long line of women waiting to speak to us, but I rushed through them to catch the name of this woman who reminded me why I'd done what I did.

When I caught up with her, I looked down at her feet to see if she still wore the Mickey Mouse socks. I guess she'd outgrown that, along with many other things.

"Thank you so much," I said, "for being so brave and for coming to find me."

"No, thank *you*," she replied. "Remember how in the beginning you said that it only takes 'one brave soul' to get the conversation started?"

"Yes," I answered.

"Well, I really wanted to be that brave soul, and you showed me how."

I hugged her, and she looked me straight in the eyes and said, "You really have a gift, Jessica. And I think God chose you especially to show people the truth. Never doubt what you're doing, because you're helping more people than you know."

At that moment, one of my actors needed my attention and tapped me on the shoulder. When I turned back around, the girl was gone. I searched for her in the throngs of young women still mingling around in the space, but I couldn't find her anywhere. She had vanished. The divine circumstances that brought us together that night make me weep to this day. If ever I needed an affirmation to keep moving forward, this was it. She represented all of the young men and women I'd listened to over the years. She was their pain, their hope, their struggle, and their success. Her story saved my life, and it inspires me every day—yet I never did catch her name.

In the end, it didn't matter what subject matter I was addressing. The hunger, desire, and need for connection and understanding made itself known. It didn't matter whether it was a male or female who spoke up or whether they were from a large city or small town—the language we all speak is universal. Whether conscious of it or not, every person who raised their hand and spoke up at one of our programs lent their voice to the collective mission to fill up on something other than our own pain, addictions, and secrets. We're all moving toward feeding our own inner hunger and filling up on life.

✳ ✳ ✳

part III

HOW TO
FILL UP
The Take-Away Tools

chapter 13

"Society Isn't Some Room Down the Hall"—
Claim Responsibility and Quit Blaming Others

Willingness is the key to changing your life. There's nothing anyone can do to help you unless you're willing to help yourself. This is a lesson that was hard for me to accept. I kept waiting for the magic pill, or the magic person who would do it all for me: love me more than I loved myself, heal me, and make me feel beautiful. I waited for those last ten pounds to come off so I could welcome my perfect, new life. Actually, I waited for the better job, better car, better man, better *anything* before I could even think of starting my life. I wanted to know the secret, the shortcut, and the easier way to do things. And anytime I did a little bit of work on myself, I wanted big results immediately. It wasn't until I was willing to let go and face the fact that I needed to do *consistent* work and take action if I was going to get anywhere that things started to shift for me. I didn't do it all or do it perfectly—I needed help and I welcomed support. But first I had to be willing to acknowledge that I desired a change. Then I had to be willing to do something about it.

I always hated the word *will* because it was attached to *willpower*—which I never thought I had due to all of my years as a yo-yo dieter. But then I took the word apart and found great inspiration in its fresh meaning. *Will* came to mean "desire of the spirit," while *power* translated to "strength of the spirit." Then I combined the two to create a new definition: To have willpower for me was to be committed to blending my spirit's desire with my spirit's strength. And so, I began to work toward something greater, instead of holding out and white-knuckling it until somebody else came along with an answer.

Realize that your life isn't going to be fixed from the outside. It won't be cured or healed by following how-to lists or articles. It won't even be better by reading books, attending seminars, or buying products. I've found that life becomes fuller when we open up, are truthful, and most of all, are willing to look inside and face the deeper issues—nothing more and nothing less. Every single one of us has an issue we're struggling with, which is why we're in "Earth school" in the first place. We can choose the way we experience these lessons, although we can't always control the way we feel about them. When we run around and try to fill ourselves up with drugs, sex, alcohol, gambling, relationships, material items, or even prestige, power, fame, and beauty, we deny ourselves a chance to use our willpower to satiate ourselves. That's why we feel empty and hollow inside.

When people ask me how I've attained the career and life I have now, I don't have a quick answer, as you can tell by experiencing my story, but I do have what I call a "toolbox for life." And in it are great, tangible, usable tools that I've collected and gathered over the years, which help me get through the day. Some of these tools have come from my own triumphs and failures, while others I've obtained from listening to people like you. The bottom line is I *use* my toolbox . . . because without it I'd be waiting to buy my happiness and progress from an infomercial.

None of my tools are guaranteed. Some days I go to my box when I'm in need, and it feels incredibly empty—I can't find one darn tool to use, and I feel stuck. Other days, I go to it and it's chock-full of instruments I use to skate through an issue. As I continue to live this life and do this work, I continue to amass tools that move me forward. In this part of the book, I'd like to share six practical, take-away tools with you that you can put in your own box and use when you're wanting—and willing—to make a change.

Blaming It

It's so tempting to believe that the root of all the pain in our lives originated from some outside force, for it's easier to believe that we have no control over our minds or our lives. For example, when I ask audiences why women feel that they have to be thin to be beautiful, why men feel they can't show emotion, or why we're all so focused on wealth and material goods; or when I ask them who teaches us that men are predators and women are victims, that it's not okay to cry, and that winning is everything, they have one answer: society.

Our bodies are not ever fully our own. Out in the world, on any given day, we can pass by thousands of images of what our heads, waists, and legs should look like. *Lean, firm, strong, sleek, tanned, and toned.* We see our breasts on billboards five stories high. We see our thighs in the "before" pictures in magazines, and we learn how our eyes can change colors and our teeth can whiten instantly. Without asking for their input, we're told by strangers that we have "Nice tits!" and a "Great ass!" Never are we treated as whole beings, people with feelings attached to those admired body parts. We're separated into pieces and we're picked apart. That just seems to be a fact. It's hard to grasp a sense of our entire selves if we're compartmentalized on a daily basis. It breaks down a human being. It's not just one advertisement, TV program, or verbal comment, but rather a steady diet of restrictive, ignorant, and hurtful images from our society that destroy a person.

Believe me, I know that *society* is a great catch-all word. For so long, I hated society for telling me that women should be skinny and pretty, that girls were supposed to grow up destroying their bodies by dieting, and that it was somehow a woman's lot in life to loathe her body. I imagined a group somewhere named "society" deciding what we see in the media and what we see on TV. But society isn't some nebulous force out there wreaking havoc on our lives, nor is it some room down the hall that holds meetings on Wednesdays. It's something all human beings are card-carrying members of. Human beings create those magazine covers, human beings pass laws that treat us unfairly, and human beings are writing and producing the TV shows we consume. It's not a machine or a faceless committee—it's *us*.

Yet while we collectively have power, the bulk of this power still lies within individual thought and action. We contribute to society every day through our actions, language, and thoughts, and until we're ready to own that, we're in a lot of trouble.

Claiming It

Claiming responsibility can be very freeing. It's up to us to raise our voices when we're able to—after all, even though horrendous things may have happened to us as children, we can't go back and fix that now. I spent the early years of my recovery blaming everyone: my parents, my teachers, my friends, my boyfriends, and the media. I got angry and felt those feelings, but then I decided that the common denominator was me. So, I could continue to hate and blame, or I could self-care and end those patterns of hurtful thoughts and behaviors. Of course it's a lot easier said than done, but the decision to take back my power and responsibility changed my life. It gave me the career and relationships I have now, and it's brought me to share my experiences with you.

Accepting responsibility for an area of your life that isn't working is so much more proactive than spending time blaming others, because being willing to claim responsibility is the first step of moving on to greater change. Owning your part of a situation—be it a fight, a belief, or a piece of gossip you've shared—is the first and biggest tool to have in your box.

When I was feeling especially frustrated with the image of women in the media, it was easy for me to say, "Well, society is to blame." But what I really had to do was dig deep and research just what went into those images. So I debunked the myths, figured out how I contributed, and brought the issue down to a level that I could understand and be willing to take action about.

For instance, most people buy a fashion or entertainment magazine without ever thinking of the industry behind it. There are hundreds of people whose job it is to manifest that magazine. Publicists pitch their clients and lobby for them to get coverage. Casting directors hire the models. Photographers spend a great deal of time lighting the space and preparing for the shoot. When the actor or model arrives, they're under construction for hours before any pictures are even taken—clothing companies have specially designed and cut clothing for them to wear; and makeup artists, hair stylists, and wardrobe people must dress and coif them. Then graphic designers airbrush the photos to get rid of any lines, blemishes, or things remotely human-looking on the model. Art directors lay the magazine out, writers create the stories, and editors check the facts. Advertisers decide what images to present in order to get readers interested in their product. The ultimate goal is to persuade you to spend your money on this magazine.

The people who work at the magazine probably aren't worrying about your feelings after you read it. They want you to believe it, and buy into the images . . . or at least buy what the model is wearing. They want you to consume because it keeps them employed. Society didn't make that magazine—people did. Wake up and realize that. If the magazine makes you feel horrible, then don't buy it. Put your money where your mouth and beliefs are. Society doesn't perpetuate images of women in provocative, sexual poses. Human beings who work in the advertising field are coming up with those images, and plenty of women are posing for them. In other words, the layers of responsibility can be staggering, and they're often not so simple. These images are acceptable and perceived as the norm because we buy into them. But just remember this: They won't sell us what we won't consume.

The biggest power you can possess is to be an educated consumer. Understand that sometimes the film in music videos is stretched to make the artists look thinner and taller. Camera and makeup tricks are employed to keep celebrities above the rest of us. It's make-believe and manufactured.

Each time you're tempted to blame someone or something else for your shortcomings, I urge you to look within. When you say—as I have in the past—that society makes you feel bad about yourself, you're letting yourself off too easy. What role do *you* play in all of this? How do you contribute to the misinformation? You may not control a hurt or a slight, but you can control the way you receive it and process it in your life.

Doing It

When we're aware and claiming responsibility, we can make a more conscious choice out in the world and, in turn, affect society greatly. Everything we do—how we drive our cars, look at other people, speak to friends, raise our children, and conduct ourselves in public—even what we think when we're alone—is part of being a contributing member of society.

We have more power than we think or are led to believe. Life with our parents gave us our first glimpses of the society we'd eventually encounter. Within that unit, we identified, created, and perpetuated a way of treating others and ourselves. We adopted a set of beliefs, and our opinions were crafted around experiences within that family unit. Now, we can choose to go through the rest of our lives living with our family's beliefs or we can establish a set for ourselves. It could be a combination of what we were raised with or it may be a complete departure—either way, we must first figure out what those beliefs are.

Every unit that we belong to is a society: schools, religious groups, circles of friends, clubs, workplaces, and so forth. I tell my university audiences to look around: Their community on campus is their society. We're also a part of a global society that we don't always see—in fact, we sometimes forget that it exists. And sometimes we can feel so powerless over something like racism, sexism, or homophobia—three current blights on the American horizon—that we may feel we can't do anything to change the injustice and hatred we see. But remember, the individual thread magnified a zillion times is what makes up the fabric of our society. Break it down to that level, and it feels less daunting.

If you don't like something that's going on out in the world, what can you do about it? Here are some take-away tools:

- Identify where this belief is coming from: Your family and friends? The peer groups on campus? The media? Be clear on where to focus your energy. Is it a corporation, an advertiser, a family member, a school event? Everything has a root cause somewhere—identify it as best you can.

- Decide what level of responsibility you wish to take. What do you want to do about it? What *can* you do? Is it something you wish to boycott? Can you write a letter, make a phone call? How willing are you to say or do something?

- Look within at what you do to perpetuate this injustice or belief. Do you speak about it in your everyday language? Do you ignore the consequences of this behavior? Do you think someone else will fix it? What do you do on a daily basis to either make it better or worse?

- Do something about it. Will it take changing a language or a belief? Will it mean committing to a volunteer effort? How far are you willing to go? Take a small action step to start. Being proactive changes the momentum and gives you back the power.

When I educated myself about what was behind the magazines I purchased, I decided that it was worth my sanity and peace to refuse to buy materials that systematically broke down my self-esteem by providing unhealthy messages. I used my money to take action, but first I got clear within myself. Now, if I do purchase a fashion or entertainment magazine, I look at it with a different set of eyes. I understand that what I see isn't real, and I know that "society" doesn't really believe I should be like those cover models.

The biggest impact we can make on our society is to walk our talk. And we need to take care of ourselves so that we may better serve others. If we spend our time just being angry or indifferent, then we only have ourselves to blame. Hearing that what we dislike most in the world could be something *we're* responsible for is hard to hear—yet understanding that in each interaction we create lies an opportunity to shift society is a very empowering tool indeed.

✳ ✳ ✳

chapter 14

"Don't Slap a Band-Aid on a Gaping Wound"—
Stop Looking for Easy Answers

There's no substitute for feeling your emotions, and there's no easy alternative for doing your personal work. The only way out of healing is *through*—through all of the pain, the questioning, the struggles, the victories, the roller coaster of life. Yet, in a country obsessed with quick fixes, we sometimes don't have the patience to watch a person in process.

One of the many things I heard from people on the road was: "We didn't talk about it in my family." The "it" didn't matter—it could have been rape, incest, bullying, fear, loneliness, happiness, dreams, self-hatred, isolation, or even everyday emotional experiences such as good grades, embarrassing schoolyard experiences, or broken hearts. The suppressed events grew into layers of unrecognized feelings that weren't released or shared, piling up to form a disease in the body, mind, and spirit. You see, the things we never get to say remain inside of us and form our perceptions of the world. There are times that what we see, feel, or experience seems unbearable and we just want to find that easy out. However, if you truly want to fill up on life, you have to be willing to go fully into the feeling of being empty.

Speaking of Fat

What's your first response when you hear someone ask, "Do I look fat in this?"

If you answered, "No," "Of course not!" or "You have such a pretty face," then you're like 99 percent of the people I talk to. Many of us have an automatic-response button installed that we hit for any question containing the word *fat*.

Men answer this question like good robots, and moms and friends spit out their responses without even thinking. These automatic replies are like Band-Aids that have been slapped on the gaping wounds of body loathing, depression, and insecurity. After all, what does it bring up for *us* when someone asks if we think they're fat? Does it make us hate them, since the people asking tend to show no visible sign of excess weight? Does it make us uncomfortable because maybe the truth is that they *have* gained a few pounds, but telling them so would be considered a social faux pas? Do we want to ask that question ourselves to get comfort, love, or encouragement?

Many of us think that people ask that question because they're looking for attention or validation. Oftentimes, women don't know how else to express what's going on for them, so they fall back on the "language of fat." Let me tell you what I mean.

When I was a freshman in college, the girls on my floor would get dressed for Saturday-night parties in front of a huge communal mirror in the hallway. We'd form a circle so that everyone could glimpse a little bit of mirror space. Then the first victim would approach the reflective wall of doubt and low self-esteem, asking the group, "You guys—I look fat, don't I?"

And without blinking a freshly mascarad eye, we'd answer, "No, you look great! Here, try my on my sweater."

The fragile girl would sit back down in the mirror circle, and the next one would approach: "You guys, I'm so ugly that I'm gonna have to drink a lot in order to hook up tonight."

And we'd say, almost in unison: "No, you're so pretty—you're totally gonna hook up tonight!"

She'd sit back down with her newly placed Band-Aid showing like a badge of courage. And we'd spend hours like this, with no one ever really speaking about what was going on inside. We were all so deathly afraid of being honest (or perhaps we just didn't know how to be) that we wasted precious time covering up our wounds instead of exposing them. We should have asked, "Why do you feel fat?" "What do you need from me?" "What's going on for you that you'd say such a thing?" but we didn't. We didn't want to know the answers—it could have gotten deep. It could have gotten emotional.

And why is it that we always want to say, "Shh, it will be okay; don't cry" when someone cries? Again, that's just another Band-Aid, one that we think is prettier and more manageable than the truth. What if it's *not* okay—what if the person wants to cry and feel and express and release? The same goes for watching someone in a bad mood and trying to snap them out of it. Snap yourself back into your *own* business, and let them feel.

When someone's going through a breakup, one of the first things we want to do is demonize the jerk who made them feel bad. We want to say, "You deserve better" or "You'll get over it." I know that as friends, we think it's our duty to always lift each other up, but it could also be a gift to let our loved ones be unfixed and unhealed as they take the time to process their emotions.

When I was visiting the schools near Columbine, I saw first-hand how everyone just wanted to put a bandage over the extreme pain that was being experienced. People wanted to point a finger, or boil all the pain down into some bite-size portion—but that doesn't work because life is big and juicy and messy. I want to chuck all of the contrite Band-Aids out the window and replace them with these actions: listening, listening, and listening.

In all fairness, we put Band-Aids on each other because we often don't know what else to do. So here are some tools that can really help:

- Listen for strong trigger words. When someone uses terms such as *hate, fat, ugly,* or *stupid* about themselves, understand that they're signifying a deeper issue that

175

they don't know how to express in another way. You
may have to ask harder questions to get them to open
up, but it isn't "normal" for people to speak like that
about themselves.

- Resist the urge to solve, fix, or heal their pain. Know that
  you must listen more than talk, and be prepared for the
  person to take their own time to heal.

- Recognize that it's okay not to have the answers. You
  don't have the responsibility to know it all.

- Try replacing Band-Aids such as "no" (which negate what
  someone has said) with "I understand you're in pain—
  what can I do?" or "What else is going on for you?" And
  then be willing to listen and go through it with them.

At first this may feel like psychobabble, but you're reworking
your expectations and then your language (more on that in the next
chapter). You're also instilling a sense of patience and grace in yourself. And keep in mind that we're all tempted to escape our
discomfort by picking at what's tangible for us: our bodies, relationships, careers, and families. But we can sometimes get cross-
addicted or obsess over an issue and transfer our discomfort in the
form of promiscuity, drug use, shopping, self-mutilation, and so on.
If we think that something easily fixable caused such deep pain,
then we're fooling ourselves.

I know that when I realized there weren't any easy answers to
these "human issues," I was bummed because that meant I had to
do some real work on myself. But now, when I'm in anguish I know
that what got me there is complex and a lesson is to be learned.
Now I do my best to ease into the healing process.

Don't be afraid—the level of connection and clarity in our relationships, which we experience by allowing our wounds to heal
properly, can save us from utter self-destruction and disconnection
later on.

chapter 15

"Change Your Words and You Change Your Life"—
Shift the Language You Use Every Day

Every word we speak holds power—the power to inspire, destroy, uplift, or damage. The energy and dynamics behind our language create the reality we live in. Words can be subtle and swift in breaking down a relationship and diminishing self-esteem, or they can be crucial in healing a crisis and rebuilding global relations. We don't spend a lot of time focusing on our language uses and abuses because words, as they say, are cheap. Or are they? We take our communications with others (and ourselves) for granted because as human beings, one of our God-given gifts is the opportunity to connect through words. Yet I believe that in order to fill up on life, we must first change our language and fill up on positive words.

Every morning when we wake up, our conversation with the world begins: "I didn't get enough done last night," or "He doesn't love me; I'm worthless." When we look in the mirror, we immediately rattle off a list of things we'd like to change: "Nose—too big; hair—too frizzy; eyes—too puffy; skin—full of zits; belly—too fat . . . " It's as if our self-esteem is already in survival mode before we've even gotten dressed!

I've learned that the way we use language and dialogue is what eventually trickles down into our everyday lives and circumstances. It forms the fundamental beginnings of our self-esteem, body-image concerns, and our capacity to build relationships. Take a moment to think about it. Right now, what are the voices in your head saying to you? If you were forced to describe yourself in three words right now, what would you say? Would the words be reflective of who you are as a person, or what you have or have not accomplished? Would they be based on your looks, style of dress, or relationship status? In other words, is the basic radio station of your self-worth programmed to easy listening or head-banging, being-hating rock?

Words That Kill

As a little girl, the language in my head was always telling me what was wrong with me. I couldn't look in the mirror and give myself the love and support I was craving. Part of my language choices came from listening to how other women around me spoke to themselves. And I absorbed that into my own psyche.

When I got older, my damaging talk became more of a mantra that I lived by—I always told myself I wasn't good enough, using hurtful words such as *ugly, fat, hideous, monster,* and *stupid.* As I consumed them on a daily basis, these poisonous words killed off any connection to a higher power or higher self I might have had. They kept me mired in hatred and negativity, and in turn, I saw this dangerous language ooze out into my relationships and life experiences.

I became increasingly addicted to the language and the attention I received when I lost weight. In a way, we're all obsessed with that first initial comment we receive after meeting someone face to face. We long to hear about how we look rather than how we make that person feel. So many times we greet someone by robotically saying, "You look great," when we could choose to tap in to the moment and say, "I'm so glad to see you!"

The response I most looked forward to receiving was, "Jessica, you look wonderful! You've lost weight!" Messages that place value on appearance ring true to the dieter. They become our drug and give us a sense of accomplishment. Now, in my recovery, this what the same message sounds like to me: "Jessica, you seem more acceptable. You take up less room in the world." Extreme, perhaps, but in reality there are a million of us out there who essentially want to disappear. We desire to become so small and insignificant that we cease to take up space.

We women bond with the language of fat. "Feeling fat" is such a common blanket term for women to express how they're feeling. But fat is *not* a feeling—it's a perceived emotional state of unhappiness, uneasiness, and desire to change. When we hear the word *fat*, we assume we know what it means to that woman.

We all allow ourselves to be bathed in dialogue that's hurtful and unhelpful. How many times during conversations with female friends have you put yourself down? Or heard them complain about their shortcomings (clothes, hair, weight)? We bond over the language we share. So what kind of quality bonding are *you* doing? Do you feel uplifted and inspired when you finish speaking with another person, or have you spent the entire time complaining, gossiping, and degrading yourself and others? Language can be the most insidious and necessary part of constructing and *decon*structing your self-esteem.

Our language informs our beliefs, ideas, and actions. For example, when dealing with an issue such as rape or assault, the way we speak about a woman absolutely contributes to the rape culture and myth: *Slut, whore, easy,* and *bitch* are all pieces of language that we hear. Where's the respect in that? Where's the honoring or protecting? Similarly, when we call a man a "player" or a "pimp," we abandon any other noble quality of what makes up a man. We say things like, "Well, he's a guy—they only thing they want to do is get laid," or "She's such a slut, she's probably making it up." This language rolls right off the tongue, as if it were no big deal—but what if bit by bit this talk broke down that person's potential?

Everyone loves a good joke. But if the jokes you tell and enjoy hearing are at the expense of others, that's something to consider.

Telling fat jokes, gay jokes, or racist jokes may seem funny at the time, but the language you use while doing so contributes to the attitudes and energy around these people. If you really want to walk your talk and see a change in the areas of fat phobia or homophobia, then stop participating in jokes that demean or belittle people in this area. Even if you're not the one telling the joke, if you're surrounded by people who do, or if you laugh and participate by listening, then you're equally responsible.

Who doesn't love a good juicy piece of gossip? Women in particular are huge culprits for gossip; we've been known to thrive on it. Hearing about someone else's struggles or foibles seems to make us feel better and takes us out of our own headspace. Gossip may seem harmless, but it can really be hurtful and disempowering. So, is it possible to refrain from spreading something you don't know to be true, even if it seems like a juicy piece of news? What would happen if you stopped bitching about someone in your life and instead were proactive and confronted them with honesty and truth? Of course it's a greater risk to do this, to use language that's affirming and positive rather than demoralizing—after all, misery loves company, and everyone loves a good bitch session. Again, I challenge us to think of a better way to connect with each other than over damaging talk.

Certainly the way we speak to each other directly impacts our lives. How many of us think nothing of telling someone off at the drop of the hat? Think about it—if someone cuts you off on the highway or in line at the bank, do you just cuss away? And when you meet up with someone, whether you're at work or at a social function, does the first thing you utter have something to do with appearance or material wealth: "Wow, you look beautiful, great haircut" or "God, I love that outfit—where did you get it?" You see, there's a difference between mindlessly offering a compliment and shifting the emphasis of your thoughts to include something more profound than whether or not somebody's hair looks nice.

Can you describe someone—be it your spouse, your best friend, or a stranger—without using a physical quality or judgment of the exterior? Are you in the practice of describing the essence of a person, or are you trained to look at the outside? Keep in mind that the way we break down other people is the same way we break down ourselves.

Language That Heals

The language you use every day is the most significant thing you can control and shift. Instead of greeting your friend with some report on how pretty or tired or sexy she looks, perhaps you could comment on her energy, her spirit, or what she does for you in your friendship: "Hey, it always makes me happy to see you" or "Your smile just lights up the room." These may seem like minor things to point out, but they'll produce major results. This simple shift reprograms your thoughts and language to focus on something greater.

In my journey as a speaker and communicator, I'm constantly struggling with and working on my language choices. It isn't enough to change them inside my head; I have to practice my new way of thinking and speaking every day. But the good news is that each day I'm given plenty of opportunities to do so. It was definitely awkward at first, but my lips and soul just had to get used to saying things differently. I make a conscious effort now to comment on a person's spirit or how they make me feel rather than their accessories. It was challenging at first, but what I uncovered and allowed by changing my language has made my life much richer and more vibrant.

Here are some take-away tools for changing your language:

- Be aware of what you say to yourself on a continual basis: What words do you choose when you describe yourself? What words would you like to use?

- What language do you use when you speak to others— is it damaging, meaningful, or honest? Do you find yourself repeating the same words over and over again, stuck in a negative pattern? Can you describe someone based on their essence?

181

- Do you engage in degrading jokes, gossip, or destructive storytelling? Watch how you describe other people—is it with care? Do you speak about the *quality* of people or stay on the surface? Can you curb your thirst for gossip or backbiting for at least one day—even one hour?

- If you're at a loss for new words that make you feel positive, try writing down a wish list of traits you admire in others. Find new options—for example, instead of commenting on someone's weight or appearance, try noting how they make you feel.

- Replace negative phrases that you might use in your own head with something else. "You're so fat," for instance, can be changed into "What can we do that's loving today?"

I'm never more saddened than when I walk into a bathroom filled with a bunch of women and find out how they feel about the size and shape of their butts before I ever know their names or what they're up to in the world. It seems like such a waste of potential to spend most of our days being negative.

Here are some adjectives that make me feel magical and alive, which I use to describe me, situations, people, and so on. There are words here that can be used to replace negative words or connotations and yet still reflect a discontentment with something, and there are words to enrich the positive vocabulary we possess: *delicious, vibrant, lovely, luscious, sensual, super-duper, empowering, radiant, zestful, important, challenging, uncomfortable, energetic, unhappy, kind, supportive, empathetic, frustrated, curvy, unique, intelligent, inspiring, yummy, healthy, ample, desirous, opportune, nontraditional, pleasing, displeased, strong, bold, powerful, encouraging, fortunate, blessed, soulful, sweet, ambitious, magical, alive, fantastic, hilarious, wounded, hopeful, committed, exuberant,* and *worthy.*

The power of the spoken word is so profound that I feel shifting and replacing your language is at the core of what it takes to change your mind and your life. Recognize that this is a process. It may not stick the first or even the 50th time. But take small steps with new language, and write down and record the difference in how it makes you and others feel. I bet you'll see an improvement!

✳ ✳ ✳

chapter 16

"Plant the Seeds and Watch Them Grow"—
Understanding Patience
and Being of Service

Cultivating patience—that is, recognizing that healing, change, and transformation don't happen overnight—is a valuable tool to have. Just like in nature, we all experience seasons of rest, growth, rebirth, and harvest. So the key to moving past our problems is to give them time, and be of service while you wait. These two components are so important to the filling-up process.

One of the craziest lessons for me to learn was that everything is always exactly as it should be. Of course I craved spiritual growth, infinite happiness, and eternal love . . . like five minutes ago. I wanted to rush through my process, find the easy answer, blame someone else, and be rescued. Unfortunately, I tried all of that and none of it worked. I had to give in to a time that wasn't my own—which was universal and divinely perfect—and that meant I had to wait.

At times, all we can do is chill out, and grasp the fact that we're not perfect. When we're willing to acknowledge that and do the necessary work, we become like farmers preparing a field for harvest. We tend to the ground by digging up the dirt, fertilizing the soil, and planting the seeds, and then we nurture those seeds with water and food. Next, we have to back off while the seeds grow. As a farmer goes off and does something else until the harvest, so should we get out of our heads by being of service to others. Whether we volunteer, call an old friend, or just listen more than we speak, when we can move out of our own "circle of stuff," it gives us perspective and respect for our own process. Then, when the timing is right, we can reap what we've planted, enjoy looking at our new growth, and take pleasure in the fact that we saw something through to completion—and then we can begin again.

Holding the Space

Most of the questions that people posed to us on the road concerned helping a loved one in trouble. When we care about someone, it's natural to want to fix, heal, nurture, and solve the problems that seem to be throwing that person off course. One mother, for instance, came up to me after a show, holding her young daughter by the wrist and begging me to tell her how to "fix my daughter from hurting herself." This girl was a cutter, and her mother was at her wit's end trying to get her to stop doing this to herself. This was an extreme case with obvious physical repercussions, and the mother was so desperate for help.

I felt this woman's pain, even as I remembered that when I was struggling with my eating disorder as a teenager, there wasn't anything another person could have told me that would have gotten through to me. Unless they were going to tell me how I could drop weight in a short period of time, I had no reason to listen. No one could love me, fix me, or heal me enough; I had to want to get help. I had to hit bottom or discover my own saturation point.

It all goes back to willingness—until a person is ready, the healing just won't happen. So what does that leave the rest of us to do in the meantime? The best thing we can do as a community is to recognize that at one time or another, one of us will be going through something. *It never stops.* The concept of a perfect world, filled with good feelings and manic emotion, is unhealthy and unrealistic. So, once we manage our expectations and swallow the fact that we're all in process, then we can assemble some patience for the natural ebb and flow of life. In other words, you should hold a space for your loved one. This doesn't mean that you're inactive or not helping—it means that you're allowing your loved one's path to emerge as it has to. It can be a challenging lesson because it requires faith. But the best thing you can do for your friend or loved one is to plant the seeds for change and wait. I know it's not the easiest advice to take, but experience has shown me that it's the most honest.

If you're dealing with someone who's struggling with an eating disorder, has been assaulted, is self-mutilating, or is abusing drugs and alcohol, here are some take-away tools that will help you plant seeds of change:

- Understand that you *cannot* fix this person. You can aid in their recovery by holding a space and being a friend, but *it's not up to you to heal them.*

- Using "I" statements, tell them what you're feeling. For example: "When I see you get drunk or high like this, it hurts because you don't act like your loving self," "It hurts me to hear you say you're fat and ugly," or "When you hurt yourself, I get scared because I don't want to lose you."

- Offer to assist them in getting outside help. Maybe you can research a local clinic, therapist, or outreach group that can offer resources to your loved one. It's good to be informed about the issue and what it takes to recover. But remember that it isn't up to you to make sure they attend a meeting or a session—you can offer to accompany them if they need you to, but don't take it all on yourself.

- Walk your talk. The best way to be a good friend is to be clear in your feelings, health, intentions, and actions. How can you help a friend who's struggling with body image when you turn around and say, "God, I have a big ass!" You must be a beacon of what you speak. The stronger and clearer you are, the better you can lead by example.

- Make sure that you're healthy enough to be a friend. This means that you don't sacrifice your own well-being for someone else. The martyr thing gets old, and it doesn't work. So mean what you say and say what you mean, and be willing to back off and let your friends do the work they need to do.

If you use these tools, your loved ones might respond as though you've just become the biggest freak on the planet. You'll be offering up an alternative to them, which may piss them off. Be prepared that they may walk away, shut down, and not speak to you for a while. That's their process to go through.

Yes, they might be angry or frustrated. Yes, they may isolate. And yes, they may be in danger. But every step of the way, you can reconfigure your plan of action, and if your gut tells you that someone is in imminent physical danger, then by all means make that emergency phone call. Listen to your intuition, but just know that in the end, you can't do the work for anyone else. Don't deny your loved one their process—or deny your own.

Being of Service

What happens when you get clear within, ditch your savior complex, clean up your language, attain valuable resource information, and employ patience in the process? This is called "planting the seeds," and you must have faith that you *will* at some point in time reap a beautiful harvest of recovery and strong relationship with your loved one. You ultimately have to decide how willing you are to stick around in the process—because one of the hardest things to experience as a mother, brother, sister, friend, or lover is watching someone you adore go through a hard time.

In the meantime, I've discovered that when we take care of ourselves, we naturally take care of others. The balance is restored. Service isn't always selfless because we rarely do anything that doesn't work for us in the end. Some call that "ego," while I just call it "human survival." I give because it makes me feel good, and it reminds me where I am, where I was, and where I'm going. I give because I see my journey on the faces of others.

I'm of service by volunteering, creating, and using my life to do work that aids in others' recovery and healing. There's no better occupation for me—I'm right where I need to be. And you can be of service every day of your life, too. Many times it will actually *save* your life by taking you out of your own misery and getting you involved in the world at large. You'll be reminded that you're not the only one struggling.

Here are some take-away tools regarding service:

- You don't have to do something grand to be of help. Listening to a friend rather than talking or making an extra phone call to check in on someone who's having a hard time is service.

- Volunteer at a place that you've benefited from—such as a hospital, clinic, school, or spiritual center. Getting out of your head and giving your time is a valuable gift, as well as a great way to stay connected.

- This one's simple but true: Remember that everyday actions and relationships cause a ripple effect out in the world, so practice being kind, and ask someone else to pass it on.

- When you're willing to be of service in your daily life—
  by giving a senior citizen a ride somewhere, explaining
  a math problem to your younger sibling, volunteering at
  an animal shelter, or smiling at a stranger—it all leaves a
  positive imprint in your wake.

One of the things I'm most proud of in my recovery is what I've
planted along the way, including inspirational friendships and a
calling to serve others. I never planned it this way: If someone
would have told me when I was 18 years old that one day I'd write
a book that spilled my guts and inner secrets to people, I would
have thought they had the wrong girl. Back then, I was a hungry,
vacant, lonely outline of who I am today. My secrets kept me
removed from healing and getting help—until one day, I decided
that I wanted a different life and was willing to do something
about it. Now, in my recovery, I've made service a big part of my
life, and I'm truly the better for it.

✳ ✳ ✳

chapter 17

"Every Moment Holds a New Choice"—
Learning How to Choose You

Many of us grew up in homes where we weren't honored or nurtured. We had experiences that left us wanting for attention, respect, or safety; and we may have lived through great abuse, strife, and misfortune. Yet no matter where we grew up or what happened to us, we have the opportunity to begin anew every day—or, rather, every moment of every day. The beliefs that we've assembled in our lives can be changed. The intense, insatiable hunger to be acknowledged, valued, and loved can lead us to believe that we must find validation outside of ourselves. But only when we choose to honor ourselves and our own needs can we begin to fill up on this self-love. There can be something very positive about being selfish, something very fulfilling about making new choices and breaking old patterns.

Taking Inventory

I met Lilly after I spoke at a community college in Atlanta. She told me that not long ago, her "disease to please" had incapacitated her, preventing her from making her own decisions. She'd constantly play out in her head how every person in her life would react to her choices—she simply couldn't imagine making a choice that would honor her own voice and needs. By looking to others, she thought she'd find her self-esteem and self-worth.

Lilly explained that she'd grown up with a mentally ill mother who went in and out of treatment for years and was never really able to be there emotionally for anyone else. Since she was an only child with no father at home, Lilly became the caretaker and parent to her own mother. She had to help her mother make tea so that she wouldn't burn herself, she had to make sure her mother took her medications, and she reminded her mother to comb her hair before she left the house. And Lilly was there when her mom would have outbursts that caused her to lose her job and sever all close relationships.

Lilly had become promiscuous at age 14 because she didn't know how to say no to attention from men. She needed to be nurtured and caressed, but instead, she sought out affection in the form of sex. For years, Lilly had given so much of herself, in all areas of her life, that she was completely empty.

When Lilly was 25, her mother died, and the years of Lilly's self-neglect finally accumulated into a life she didn't want to live. Her hatred for her promiscuity and even her mother's illness had led her to bury her feelings in food and alcohol. Lilly knew that her life was leading her down a dead-end street—she just didn't know what to do about it.

She said that it had been scary to think about herself, but she began by spending some time writing down what her own opinions were in a journal, and then comparing them to her mother's. Lilly needed to make a clean break and figure out what her own thoughts were, so she wrote about *everything*—from how she liked to wash a car to the best way to apply for a job. She went through her belief system and took an inventory to assess where her voice was. She had to break down all of her old family patterns and create new choices for her adult life—choices that would support what her current needs were. Eventually she realized that she barely knew how to help herself, so she sought help from a therapist.

Lilly said, "I didn't know how to choose me even if there was no one else left to pick from," but she'd discovered that the opportunity to choose herself came up many times during the day. It could be as simple as deciding what kind of food she wanted to eat or learning to say no to a colleague who wanted to meet her for coffee. At first, Lilly had a very difficult time with this and fell back into rituals of pleasing others, but slowly she began to turn her life around. She had to keep "practicing" by always taking an inventory of what her thoughts were, but with each little step, she grew stronger and became more insightful about the woman she was becoming.

As you can see by Lilly's example, the only way to choose *you* is to know yourself. This takes time, practice, and patience. Every moment holds a new choice, a new opportunity to change. If you keep telling the story of your life as a victim, it will render you powerless. Realize that in the course of a day, there are scores of new choices to make that can shift and change the momentum of your life.

Be Willing to Choose

Leaning when to say no and yes to situations can make a difference in how you choose yourself. Many of us share with Lilly the desire to please others and make them happy, sometimes at the expense of our own sanity and well-being. Sometimes saying no to a date or job opportunity can serve to hold a space for something better to come along. Saying no when it really honors your spirit is the most freeing and challenging thing you can do; saying yes can be equally as thrilling, because if spoken to uphold your heart's desire, it can unleash a world of possibility.

Releasing the notion that you have to do anything perfectly will also help you choose yourself and allow your process to unfold. You're going to make mistakes along the way—you'll eat what you don't really want to, think what you shouldn't think, or act in a destructive way fashion. What's so great in living for today, being in the present moment, and being willing to do the footwork is that in every moment you have a chance to do it all over again, to choose you.

Here are some take-away tools for remembering to choose you:

- Assess your own belief system. Discover if you're taking on others' viewpoints or giving yourself an opportunity to craft your own. Try writing down an opinion inventory, which can be broad and basic, silly or deep: What are your thoughts on friendship, political issues, or even doing the laundry? You may be amazed to discover that you have different opinions than your parents or friends do.

- Be willing to let go what doesn't serve you anymore. At one point, you did things because they served a purpose—you stayed in relationships that weren't healthy or treated yourself in a way that kept you removed from others and numb. And your family patterns don't need to be carried over into your adult life unless you want them to.

- Try these new ways on, and be willing to practice. It may mean changing your language so that you don't use degrading words anymore. It may mean being more conscious of judging and gossiping about others. It may mean not engaging in negative body talk with friends. You need to *practice* these changes and be patient in the process.

- Replenish and renew! By treating yourself with more loving kindness, you'll foster a connection that helps you get closer to your truth. Massages, days off, keeping a journal—anything that allows you to spend time with yourself is beneficial.

Anything worth changing takes time, which was a challenging concept for me to grasp, since I not only suffer from the disease to please but also from perfectionism. What was freeing for me was to realize that I don't have to do *anything* perfectly, and I get a lot

194

of opportunities throughout each day to practice choosing me. I might blow it and react to a friend inappropriately, but the great news is that I can either make amends to that person right away, or I can apply what I just learned in the next interaction. I can only do this by being conscious and willing to choose me.

I still have a difficult time accepting that I may have to disappoint others to be true to myself. I worry that I'll be letting someone else down if I make a selfish decision. But I've found that when I'm being honest and loving to myself, then any decision I make will ultimately be honest and loving to all of those involved.

The way that we're going to fill up on life and make a greater change in the world is to recognize that we have to walk our talk, which we can do by living in integrity. The path toward feeling and acting worthy begins by choosing to honor, protect, and respect ourselves. It's no one else's job to do. The greatest gift we get, in every moment of every day, is the chance to make a new choice.

✳ ✳ ✳

chapter 18

"Speak Up, Speak Out"—
Leaving a Legacy
of Change

Over the course of your lifetime, you'll add and subtract many of the tools in your "toolbox for life"—you'll need stronger and more advanced ones, and you may need to throw out the entire box and start again. That's called *progress*. How many or what kind of tools you're going to need to help you cope out there in the world can't be answered by me or anyone else, but what's for certain is that they won't do anything for you unless you use them. You can't build a house by just looking at a hammer. So will you choose to use your tools to plant seeds of change, hope, and inspiration?

We need to replace our attitudes about this kind of work—it doesn't have to consist of laborious bitch sessions filled with self-help clichés. Instead, we can view doing the work with these tools as a great expression of self-respect, because when we take care of ourselves, we can take care of others.

What are you giving back to the world? What individual legacies will you leave behind? What sort of living memories will you create with those around you? Many of the people I've met on my journey have been moved to give back what they've learned in their lives. In other words, it's in the *doing* that healing happens. Some say that action is the most important prayer. What moves us into action can come in all shapes and sizes—it can be a conversation, a hug, a look in the eye, a continual social injustice, or a national tragedy. Looking back, I see that my life and work kept getting created together. The fuel I needed in my life came from listening and talking to other people. It was the foundation of my recovery from an eating disorder, and it's the cornerstone of my being in the world today.

Giving service and seeing the seeds I've planted turn into beautiful life-giving opportunities make me proud to be who I am. This has transcended my body shape or size, overcome hurtful childhood memories, and outlasted outdated notions of what a woman should be like.

It Just Takes One Brave Soul

If we look back at all of the social movements in our country's history, we can see that they only needed the sparks of individuals to ignite sweeping infernos of change. It took the brave souls who were moved or forced into action to provide a chance for us all to move forward. Nothing less has been happening in the schools and communities that I've been a part of. I've seen small changes and large ones, too. I've seen young people start activist groups on campus, recognizing that their futures lie in taking a stand and not shutting up. I've seen traditions bend and fall apart because just one person spoke up. I've seen great change in the private lives of my audience, in the way that they conduct a dialogue with themselves and in their relationships. I've seen people graduate with degrees they thought they'd never have.

You don't have to be skilled or trained in activism and outreach to do your part. The only requirement is the desire to see a change and the risk to stand alone. Because sometimes you will. Going against the grain and walking upstream isn't the easiest choice to make, but if you're inclined to try your hand at instituting social change and being of service, here are some take-away tools to use:

- Write either a letter or e-mail. This is still a powerful way to get your message across. It only takes a few minutes to make a great impact. Find out who's responsible for the issue at hand and let them know how you feel. Don't assume that someone else is writing that letter, or that it has to be perfect. Just write with your heart and passion.

- Put your money where your heart is. The almighty dollar is the leveling tool to use when wanting to institute change. You may not be a big, powerful corporation or a wealthy family, but you can spend your money responsibly and proactively. Combine tool one and two and write to the person or company to let them know that you're not spending your money to support them.

- Be proactive in your everyday life. Find ways to apply what you're passionate about in your daily experiences. If you feel that the world places too much emphasis on beauty, then you can choose to counteract that by not engaging in that dialogue with others. Or if you feel that people aren't kind enough to the homeless, then get educated on what you can do to help. You can make monumental changes in your life by putting your beliefs into practice.

- Choose to protest. Messages are sent to the world at large by creating events that let others know you've had enough. When we protested the Mifflin Mob for all those years, we never really dreamed we could stop a 20-year-old tradition. But we did. Gather like-minded souls, plan a strategy, and let your voices ring out. Please remember that hurting others isn't the way to get your point across—there are ways to protest strongly and safely. (You can see the MTV clip of our activism in action at **www.jessicaweiner.com.**)

- Create "Speak Out" groups on your campus and in your community. Like a book club, you can bring other people together who wish to talk about the issues, and you can plan events around topics you're passionate about. This is a good way to discuss things that may be affecting your community, and it's also a good way to raise consciousness within your school. You can also sign up for a "Speak Out" group on my Website.

- Volunteer! There are many understaffed and necessary social groups and programs out there that need your help. Investigate what cause you might want to get involved with and offer your time and energy. There's always work to be done.

- Start your own program. Remember that I started Youth and the Arts as a way to bring art and creativity to children who wouldn't normally be exposed to it. So if you feel that you can help fill a void by creating a new social program, do it! You can even get started on a small level on your campus or in your workplace.

- Get creative. Use your unique voice or talent to give back to the world. Your active outreach may not be created yet, so think outside the box and do something different. Find a way to combine the things you love and are passionate about to provide a service to humanity.

- Take a risk. No matter what you end up doing, commit to being heard. You may have to stand alone for a while, but the squeaky wheel gets the grease. You have to decide just how important it is to see a change. Waiting around for someone else to do the work will make you complacent and keep you stuck—great change comes from risk takers.

- Walk your talk. No matter how much you protest, write letters, or start programs, you still have the responsibility to take up space in the world as a healthy, active, truthful, loving human being. The best tool is still to integrate these principles in all of your affairs.

Choosing to Feel Full

Mine could be the story of an accidental healing that turned into a career and life mission. I had no plans to do any of this. I was simply willing to follow my journey toward health and connection—I never dreamed I could make a living at it. But you can. Being active and participating in social movements can also pay your bills. You can create your own career path. It took lots of risk and support from my family, but if I can do it, so can you. I used to be so concerned with blending in and being smaller and unseen. Now I'm reveling in the fact that I stick out and am heard!

Like me, the men and women I've met while traveling across this country are hungry—for leadership, guidance, and monumental change. We want to speak up and speak out about the things that have happened in our lives. We want to abolish the shame attached to hardships such as addiction, abuse, eating disorders, and depression. We want to move beyond the material goods being pushed down our throats, and we want to reestablish the morals, values, and parameters we live in. We want to be of service, make a difference, and institute change.

Yet there seems to be this lack of knowing that there's another way to do things. The world is undoubtedly changing, and the more time we spend on surface issues, the more we're distracted from being participants in the next generation. We want to know that our voices are being heard, but first we have to find our voices. Then we have to use them.

We *can* become filled up with power, ideas, and movement toward change . . . filled up with the knowledge that we're worth getting healthy, reaching out, and loving others . . . filled up with the understanding that if we don't take responsibility for our own lives and the world we wish to create, then no one else will. We can enjoy our own journeys and relish the people we're becoming. We can raise the bar, make new rules, live outside the box, and change the world.

Using our tools for change, we can move through our lessons with greater serenity. By not being afraid to look inside and feel our emotions deeply, by recognizing that everyone has the right to be different and unique, by choosing ourselves and looking out for others, by being willing to do the work and take the risks, and by creating small steps and moving giant leaps, we can fill up on life. And when we're full of life, we don't have to be hungry for anything anymore.

✳ ✳ ✳

afterword

In working on this book, I saw my own journey twist and turn in and out of darkness and struggle. There were many moments when I wanted to run away from writing my truth because it was painful, vulnerable, embarrassing, and almost too honest. It's so tempting to feel "not good enough" and to let that negativity derail you from your purpose. When I was doubting my ability to write this book, I got a lot of "God Shots," as I call them, or moments that specifically let me know I'm not alone. For example, I'd receive an e-mail or letter from a woman who had been at a session months earlier, telling me how she's walking her talk and seeing change in her life. She'd write to me at the exact moment I was doubting myself, and her words of thanks and encouragement helped to lift me up and get me back on track.

I need to be reminded, too—after all, I'm no better or worse than anyone else. We're all one and the same, slowly and imperfectly moving our way toward growth and the truth.

Many of you have asked me how you can do this kind of work as well. As you can see from my story, I made most of it up as I moved through my life. There was no master plan. The only thing that never wavered was my vision for making a difference. You can do the same.

I marvel at the woman I'm becoming, and I want to thank you for giving me a space to be . . . me. I'm a work in progress, so my story and words aren't a substitute for your own journeys and experiences. If something inside of you is being stirred from this work and you need more attention or help, then please seek the appropriate resources in your area. You're worth it.

As I proceed on my journey, bringing this work to a larger audience through TV, books, and so forth, there's one thing I'm certain of: I'm going to continue to show up and share what I'm learning with you, and I ask the same of you. Together we'll create magic and miracles.

I am alive, and in awe of the possibility inside all of us!

self-help resources

The following list of resources can be used to access information on a variety of issues. The addresses and telephone numbers listed are for the national headquarters; look in your local Yellow Pages under "Community Services" for resources closer to your area.

In addition to the following groups, other self-help organizations may be available in your area to assist your healing and recovery for a particular life crisis not listed here. Consult your telephone directory, call a counseling center or help line near you, or contact:

AIDS

(United States)

CDC National AIDS Hotline
(800) 342-2437

Caring for Babies with AIDS
P.O. Box 35135
Los Angeles, CA 90035
(323) 931-9828
www.caring4babieswithaids.org

Children with AIDS (CWA)
Project of America
P.O. Box 23778
Tempe, AZ 85285
(800) 866-AIDS (24-hour hotline)
www.aidskids.org

Elizabeth Glaser Pediatric AIDS
Foundation
2950 31st St., #125
Santa Monica, CA 90405
(888) 499-HOPE (4673)
www.pedaids.org

The Names Project Foundation—
AIDS Memorial Quilt
P.O. Box 5552
Atlanta, GA 31107
(800) 872-6263
www.aidsquilt.org

Project Inform
205 13th St., Ste. 2001
San Francisco, CA 94103
(800) 822-7422 (treatment hotline)
(415) 558-9051 (S.F. and Intl.)
www.projectinform.org

Spanish HIV/STD/AIDS Hotline
(800) 344-7432

TTY (Hearing Impaired) AIDS Hotline
(CDC National HIV/AIDS)
(800) 243-7889

(United Kingdom)

National AIDS Helpline
0 800 567123
www.healthwise.org.uk

National AIDS Trust
New City Cloisters
196 Old Street
London EC1V 9F4
020 7814 6767
www.nat.org.uk

(Canada)

Canadian AIDS Society
4th Floor—309 rue Cooper Street
Ottawa ON K2P 0G5
(613)230-3580
Health Canada
HIV/AIDS
www.aidsida.com

ALCOHOL ABUSE

(United States)

Al-Anon Family Group Headquarters
1600 Corporate Landing Parkway
Virginia Beach, VA 23454-5617
(888) 4AL-ANON
www.al-anon.alateen.org

205

Alcoholics Anonymous (AA)
General Service Office
475 Riverside Dr., 11th Floor
New York, NY 10115
(212) 870-3400
www.alcoholics-anonymous.org

Children of Alcoholics Foundation
164 W. 74th St.
New York, NY 10023
(800) 359-COAF
www.coaf.org

Mothers Against Drunk Driving (MADD)
P.O. Box 541688
Dallas, TX 75354
(800) GET-MADD (438-6233)
www.madd.org

**National Association of Children of
Alcoholics (NACoA)**
11426 Rockville Pike, #100
Rockville, MD 20852
(301) 468-0985
(888) 554-2627
www.nacoa.net

**National Clearinghouse for
Alcohol and Drug Information (NCADI)**
P.O. Box 2345
Rockville, MD 20847
(800) 729-6686
www.health.org

**National Council on Alcoholism and
Drug Dependence (NCADD)**
20 Exchange Pl., Ste. 2902
New York, NY 10005
(212) 269-7797
(800) NCA-CALL (24-hour hotline)
www.ncadd.org

Women for Sobriety
P.O. Box 618
Quakertown, PA 18951
(215) 536-8026
www.womenforsobriety.org

(United Kingdom)

Alcohol Concern
020 7922 8667
www.alcoholconcern.org.uk

Alcoholics Anonymous
General Service Office
P.O. Box 1, Stonebow House
Stonebow YO1 7NJ
(44) 01904-644026
www.alcoholics-anonymous.org.uk

Healthwise Drinkline
0800 917 8282
www.healthwise.org.uk

(Canada)

Alcoholics Anonymous
www.aa.org/index.html

Al-Anon/Alateen
(800) 714-7498 (for information
and materials)
(800) 443-4525 (for meeting locations)

Canadian Center on Substance Abuse
75 Albert Street, Ste. 300
Ottawa ON K1P 5E7
(613) 235-4048
www.ccsa.ca

Canadians for Safe and Sober Driving
P.O. Box 397
Station "A"
Brampton ON L6V 2L3
(905) 793-4233
www.add.ca

ALZHEIMER'S DISEASE

(United States)

Alzheimer's Association
919 N. Michigan Ave., Ste. 1100
Chicago, IL 60611
(800) 272-3900
www.alz.org

**Alzheimer's Disease Education
and Referral Center**
P.O. Box 8250
Silver Spring, MD 20907
(800) 438-4380
adear@alzheimers.org

Eldercare Locator
330 Independence Ave., SW
Washington, DC 20201
(800) 677-1116
www.eldercare.gov

The Leeza Gibbons Memory Foundation
3050 Biscayne Blvd., Suite 908
Miami, FL 33137
(818) 972-8899
www.memorycenters.com

(United Kingdom)

Alzheimer's Society
Gordon House
10 Greencoat Place
London SW1P 1PH
020 7606 0606
www.alzheimers.org.uk

Alzheimer Society of Canada
20 Eglinton Avenue W., Suite 1200
Toronto ON M4R 1K8
(800) 616-8816
www.alzheimer.ca

CANCER

(Unites States)

National Cancer Institute
(800) 4-CANCER
www.nci.nih.gov

(United Kingdom)

CancerHelp UK
Institute for Cancer Studies
University of Birmingham
Edgbaston
Birmingham B15 2TA
www.cancerhelp.org.uk

(Canada)

Canadian Cancer Society
(888) 939-3333
www.cancer.ca

CHILDREN'S ISSUES

Child Molestation

(United States)

Childhelp USA/Child Abuse Hotline
15757 N. 78th St.
Scottsdale, AZ 85260
(800) 422-4453
www.childhelpusa.org

Prevent Child Abuse America
200 South Michigan Ave., 17th Floor
Chicago, IL 60604
(312) 663-3520
www.preventchildabuse.org

(United Kingdom)

Childline
Royal Mail Building, 2nd Floor
Studd Street
London N1 OQW
0800 1111 (helpline)
0800 400 222 (text phone service)
www.childline.org.uk

National Society for the Prevention of Cruelty to Children (NSPCC)
Weston House

42 Curtains Road
London EC2A 3NH
020 7825 2500 (administration)
0808 800 5000 (helpline)

(Canada)

Child Abuse Hotline
(800) 387-5437

Kids Help Phone
(800) 668-6868
http://kidshelp.simaptico.ca

The Canadian Society for the Prevention of Cruelty to Children
Box 700, 356 First Street
Midland ON L4R 4P4
(705)526-5647

Crisis Intervention

(United States)

Girls and Boys Town National Hotline
(800) 448-3000
www.boystown.org

Children of the Night
14530 Sylvan St.
Van Nuys, CA 91411
(800) 551-1300
www.childrenofthenight.org

Covenant House Hotline
(800) 999-9999
www.covenanthouse.org

Kid Save Line
(800) 543-7283
www.kidspeace.org

Youth Nineline
(referrals for parents/teens about drugs, homelessness, runaways)
(800) 999-9999

(United Kingdom)

Barnardo's
Tanner's Lane
Barkingside
Ilford IG6 1QG
020 8550 8822
www.barnardos.org.uk

Childline
Royal Mail Building, 2nd Floor
Studd Street
London N1 OQW
0800 1111 (helpline)
0800 400 222 (text phone service)
www.childline.org.uk

A VERY HUNGRY GIRL

The Prince's Trust
18 Park Square East
London NW1 4LH
020 7543 1234
www.princes-trust.org.uk

Safe in the City
020 7922 5710
www.safeinthecity.org.uk

(Canada)

Covenant House
575 Drake Street
Vancouver BC V6B 4K8
(604) 685-7474
www.covenenthousebc.org

Covenant House
20 Gerrard Street East
Toronto, ON M5B 2P3
(416) 598-4898
www.covenanthouse.org

Kids Help Phone
(800) 668-6868
http://kidshelp.simpatico.ca

Missing Children

(United States)

Missing Children . . . HELP Center
410 Ware Blvd., Ste. 710
Tampa, FL 33619
(800) USA-KIDS
www.800usakids.org

National Center for Missing &
Exploited Children
699 Prince St.
Alexandria, VA 22314
(800) 843-5678 (24-hour hotline)
www.missingkids.org

(United Kingdom)

National Missing Persons Helpline
0500 700 700
www.missingpersons.org

UK Missing and Exploited Children
http://uk.missingkids.com

(Canada)

Child Find Canada
1-1808 Main Street
Winnipeg MB R2V 2A3
(204) 339-5584
www.childfind.ca

Missing Children Society of Canada
Suite 219, 3501 - 23 Street NE

Calgary AB T2E 6V8
(800) 661-6160
www.mcsc.ca

Children with Serious Illnesses
(fulfilling wishes):
(United States)

Brass Ring Society
National Headquarters
551 E. Semoran Blvd., Ste. E-5
Fern Park, FL 32730
(407) 339-6188
(800) 666-WISH
www.worldramp.net/brassring

Make-a-Wish Foundation
3550 N. Central Ave., Ste. 300
Phoenix, AZ 85012
(800) 722-WISH (9474)
www.wish.org

(United Kingdom)

Make-a-Wish Foundation UK
01276 24127
www.make-a-wish.org.uk

Starlight Foundation
11-15 Emerald Street
London WC1N 3QL
020 7430 1642
www.starlight.org.uk

(Canada)

Make-a-Wish Foundation of Canada
2239 Oak Street
Vancouver BC V6H 3W6
(888) 822-9474
www.makeawish.ca

CO-DEPENDENCY

Co-Dependents Anonymous
P.O. Box 33577
Phoenix, AZ 85067
(602) 277-7991
www.codependents.org

Co-Dependents Anonymous
World Service, Inc.
P.O. Box 7051
Thomaston, GA USA 30286-0025
(706) 648-6868
www.wscoda.org

DEATH/GRIEVING/SUICIDE

(United States)

AARP Grief and Loss Programs

208

(202) 434-2260
(800) 424-3410
www.aarp.org/griefandloss

Grief Recovery Institute
P.O. Box 6061-382
Sherman Oaks, CA 91413
(818) 907-9600
www.grief-recovery.com

National Hospice and Palliative Care Organization
1700 Diagonal Rd., Ste. 300
Alexandria, VA 22314
(703) 837-1500
www.nhpco.org

Parents of Murdered Children
(recovering from violent death of friend or
family member)
100 E 8th St., Ste. B41
Cincinnati, OH 45202
(513) 721-5683
(888) 818-POMC
www.pomc.com

**SIDS (Sudden Infant Death
Syndrome) Alliance**
1314 Bedford Ave., Ste. 210
Baltimore, MD 21208
(800) 221-7437
www.sidsalliance.org

**Suicide Awareness Voices of
Education (SAVE)**
Minneapolis, MN 55424
(952) 946-7998

Suicide National Hotline
(800) 784-2433

(United Kingdom)

The Compassionate Friends
53 North Street
Bristol BS3 1EN
0117 953 9639 (helpline)
0177 966 5202 (administration)
www.compassionatefriends.org.uk

Winston's Wish
The Clara Burgess Centre
Gloucestershire Royal Hospital
Great Western Road
Gloucester GL1 3NN
+44 (0) 1452 394377 (general inquiries)
0845 20 30 40 5 (family line)
www.winstonswish.org.uk

(Canada)

Canadian Hospice Palliative Care Association
43 Bruyère St., Ste. 131 C
Ottawa, ON K1N 5C8
(800) 668-2785
www.cpa.net

Seasons Centre for Grieving Children
4 Alliance Boulevard, Unit 7
Barrie ON L4M 5J1
(705) 721-5437
www.seasonscentre.com

Suicide Information and Education Centre
#201 1615-10th Avenue SW
Calgary AB T3C 0J7
www.suicideinfo.ca

DEBTS

(United States)

**Consumer Credit Counseling Service
Credit Referral**
(800) 388-CCCS

Debtors Anonymous
General Service Office
P.O. Box 920888
Needham, MA 02492-0009
(781) 453-2743
www.debtorsanonymous.org

DIABETES

(United States)

American Diabetes Association
(800) 342-2383
www.diabetes.org

(United Kingdom)

Diabetes UK
10 Parkway
London NW1 7AA
020 7424 1000
www.diabetesuk.org

(Canada)

Canadian Diabetes Association
(800) 226-8464
www.diabetes.ca

DOMESTIC VIOLENCE

(United States)

National Coalition Against Domestic Violence
P.O. Box 18749
Denver, CO 80218
(303) 831-9251
www.ncadv.org

National Domestic Violence Hotline
P.O. Box 161810
Austin, TX 78716
(800) 799-SAFE (24-hour hotline)

(800) 787-3224 (TTY)
www.ndvh.org

(United Kingdom)

Women's Aid
P.O. Box 391
Bristol BS99 7WS
08457 023 468 (helpline)
0117 944 441 (administration)
www.womensaid.org.uk

Victim Support
0845 30 30 900 (helpline)

(Canada)

Evolve (KLINIC)
870 Portage Ave.
Winnipeg, MB MR3G 0P1
(204) 784-4090
www.klinic.mb.ca
National Domestic Violence Hotline
(800) 363-9010

Safe Home
(888) 926-0301

DRUG ABUSE

(United States)

**Cocaine Anonymous National
Referral Line**
(800) 347-8998

National Helpline of Phoenix House
(cocaine abuse hotline)
(800) 262-2463
(800) COCAINE
www.drughelp.org

National Institute of Drug Abuse (NIDA)
6001 Executive Blvd., Rm. 5213
Bethesda, MD 20892-9561
Parklawn Building
(301) 443-6245 (for information)
(800) 662-4357 (for help)
www.nida.nih.gov

World Service Office, Inc.
3740 Overland Ave., Ste. C
Los Angeles, CA 90034-6337
(310) 559-5833

(United Kingdom)

National Drug Helpline
0800 77 66 00
www.ndhl.org.uk

**The Centre for Recovery
Cyswllt Ceredigion Contact**

49 North Parade
Ceredigion SY23 2JN
01970 626470
www.recovery.org.uk

Narcotics Anonymous—UK Region
020 7730 0009
www.ukna.org

(Canada)

Canadian Assembly Narcotics Anonymous
CANA/ACNA
P.O. Box 25073 RPO West Kildonan
Winnipeg MB R2V 4C7
www.cana-acna.org

Canadian Centre on Substance Abuse
75 Albert St., Ste. 300
Ottawa ON K1P 5E7
(613) 235-4048
www.ccsa.ca

EATING DISORDERS

(United States)

Overeaters Anonymous
National Office
P.O. Box 44020
Rio Rancho, NM 87174-4020
(505) 891-2664
www.overeatersanonymous.org

(United Kingdom)

Eating Disorders Association
103 Prince of Wales Road
Norwich NR1 1DW
0845 634 1414 (adults)
0845 634 7650 (youth)
www.edauk.com

(Canada)

National Eating Disorder Information Center
CW 1- 211 Elizabeth Street
Toronto, ON M5G 2C4
(866) 633-4240
www.nedic.ca

GAMBLING

Gamblers Anonymous
International Service Office
P.O. Box 17173
Los Angeles, CA 90017
(213) 386-8789
www.gamblersanonymous.org

Gamblers Anonymous UK
P.O. Box 88

London SW10 0EU
08700 50 88 80
www.gamblersanonymous.org.uk

Gamblers Anonymous Canada
(by Province)
www.gamlersanonymous.org.mtgdirCAN.html

HEALTH ISSUES

(United States)

American Chronic Pain Association
P.O. Box 850
Rocklin, CA 95677
(916) 632-0922
www.theacpa.org

American Holistic Health Association
P.O. Box 17400
Anaheim, CA 92817
(714) 779-6152
www.ahha.org

The Chopra Center
Deepak Chopra, M.D.
2013 Costa del Mar
Carlsbad, CA 92009
(760) 931-7524
www.chopra.com

The Fetzer Institute
9292 West KL Ave.
Kalamazoo, MI 49009
(616) 375-2000
www.fetzer.org

Hippocrates Health Institute
(A favorite annual retreat for Louise Hay)
1443 Palmdale Court
West Palm Beach, FL 33411
(800) 842-2125
www.hippocratesinst.com

Hospicelink
190 W. Brook Rd.
Essex, CT 06426
(800) 331-1620

Institute for Noetic Sciences
101 San Antonio Rd.
Petaluma, CA 94952
(707) 775-3500
www.noetic.org

The Mind-Body Medical Institute
110 Francis St., Ste. 1A
Boston, MA 02215
(617) 632-9530 (press 1)
www.mbmi.org

National Health Information Center
P.O. Box 1133
Washington, DC 20013-1133

(800) 336-4797
www.health.gov/NHIC

Optimum Health Institute
(Louise Hay loves this place!)
6970 Central Ave.
Lemon Grove, CA 91945
(619) 464-3346
www.optimumhealth.org

Preventive Medicine Research Institute
Dean Ornish, M.D.
900 Bridgeway, Ste. 2
Sausalito, CA 94965
(415) 332-2525
www.pmri.org

(United Kingdom)

National Health Service (NHS) Direct
0845 4647 (24-hour nurse advice line)
www.nhsdirect.nhs.uk

UK Health Centre
www.healthcentre.org.uk

(Canada)

Health Canada
Minister's Office
Brooke Claxton Bldg., Tunney's Pasture
PL 0906C
Ottawa, ON K1A 0K9
(613) 952-1154 (fax)
www.hc-sc.gc.ca

HOUSING RESOURCES

(United States)

Acorn
(nonprofit network of low- and
moderate-income housing)
739 8th St., S.E.
Washington, DC 20003
(202) 547-9292

(United Kingdom)

The Abbeyfield Society (for elderly people)
The Abbeyfield House
53 Victoria St.
St Albans
Herts AL1 3UW
01727 857536
www.abbeyfield.com

Centrepoint (for young people)
Neil House
7 Whitechapel Road
London E1 1DU
020 7426 5300
www.centrepoint.org.uk

Shelterline
0808 8000 4444
www.shelter.org.uk

(Canada)

Abbeyfield Houses Society of Canada
Box 1, 427 Bloor St. West
Toronto, ON M5S 1X7
(416) 920-7483
www.abbeyfield.ca

Canada Mortgage and Housing Corporation
700 Montreal Rd.
Ottawa, ON K1A 0P7
(613) 748-2000
www.cmhc-schl.gc.ca

IMPOTENCE

(United States)

Impotence Institute of America
8201 Corporate Dr., Ste. 320
Landover, MD 20715
(800) 669-1603
www.impotenceworld.org

(United Kingdom)

The Impotence Association
P.O. Box 10296
London SW17 9WH
020 8767 7791
www.impotence.org.uk

MENTAL HEALTH

(United States)

American Psychiatric Association of America
1400 "K" St. NW
Washington, DC 20005
(888) 357-7924
www.psych.org

Anxiety Disorders Association of America
11900 Parklawn Dr., Ste. 100
Rockville, MD 20852
(301) 231-9350
www.adaa.org

The Help Center of the American Psychological Association
(800) 964-2000
www.helping.apa.org

The International Society for Mental Health Online
www.ismho.org

Knowledge Exchange Network
www.mentalhealth.org

National Center for Post-Traumatic Stress Disorder (PTSD)
(802) 296-5132
www.ncptsd.org

National Alliance for the Mentally Ill
2107 Wilson Blvd., Ste. 300
Arlington, VA 22201
(800) 950-6264
www.nami.org

National Depressive and Manic-Depressive Association
730 N. Franklin St., Ste. 501
Chicago, IL 60610
(800) 826-3632
www.ndmda.org

National Institute of Mental Health
6001 Executive Blvd.
Room 8184, MSC 9663
Bethesda, MD 20892
(301) 443-4513
(301) 443-8431 (TTY)
www.nimh.nih.gov

(United Kingdom)

Mind (The National Association for Mental Health)
15-19 Broadway
London E15 4BQ
020 8519 2122
www.mind.org.uk

Sane
1st Floor
Cityside House
40AdlerStreet
London E1 1EE
020 7375 1002
0845 767 8000 (saneline—open noon–2 A.M.)
www.sane.org.uk

(Canada)

Canadian Mental Health Association
2160 Yonge Street, 3rd Floor
Toronto, ON M4S 2Z3
(416) 484-7750
www.cmha.ca

Mood Disorders Association of Canada
4-1000 Notre Dame Ave.
Winnipeg, MB R3E 0N3
(800) 263-1460

PET BEREAVEMENT

(United States)

Bide-A-Wee Foundation
410 E. 38th St.
New York, NY 10016
(212) 532-6395

Grief Recovery Hotline
(800) 445-4808

Holistic Animal Consulting Centre
29 Lyman Ave.
Staten Island, NY 10305
(718) 720-5548

(United Kingdom)

Animal Samaritans
52 Verdant Lane
London SE3 1LF
020 8852 9132
www.animalsamaritans.org.uk

(Canada)

Pet Therapy Society of Northern Alberta
330, 9768 170 Street
Edmonton, AB T5T L54
(780) 413-4682
http://paws.shopalberta.com/PTRemember.htm

RAPE/SEXUAL ISSUES

(United States)

Rape, Abuse, and Incest National Network
(800) 656-4673
www.rainn.org

SafePlace
P.O. Box 19454
Austin, TX 78760
(512) 440-7273

National Council on Sexual Addictions and Compulsivity
P.O. Box 725544
Atlanta, GA 31139
(770) 541-9912
www.ncsac.org

Sexually Transmitted Disease Referral
(800) 227-8922

(United Kingdom)

Rape Crisis Federation of Wales and England
7 Mansfield Rd.
Nottingham NG1 3FB
0115 934 8474
www.rapecrisis.co.uk

Rape and Sexual Abuse Counseling
01962 848018 (administration)
01962 848024 (helpline for women)
01962 848027 (helpline for men)
http://rasc.org.uk

(Canada)

Canadian Association of Sexual Assault Centres
77 East 20th Ave.
Vancouver BC V5V 1L7
(604) 876-2622
www.casac.ca

Let's Protect
(list of resources for women in Canada and the U.S.)
www.letsprotect.com

SMOKING

(United States)

Nicotine Anonymous World Services
419 Main St., PMB #370
Huntington Beach, CA 92648
(415) 750-0328
www.nicotine-anonymous.org

(United Kingdom)

Quit
0800 00 22 00
www.quit.org.uk

(Canada)

Lung Association
3 Raymond St., Ste. 300
Ottawa ON KR1 1A3
(613) 569-6411
www.lung.ca/smoking

STRESS REDUCTION

(United States)

The Biofeedback & Psychophysiology Clinic
The Menninger Clinic
P.O. Box 829
Topeka, KS 66601-0829
(800) 351-9058
www.menninger.edu

New York Open Center
(In-depth workshops to invigorate the spirit)
83 Spring St.
New York, NY 10012
(212) 219-2527
www.opencenter.org

Omega Institute
(a healing, spiritual retreat community)
150 Lake Dr.
Rhinebeck, NY 12572-3212
(845) 266-4444 (info)
(800) 944-1001 (to enroll)
www.eomega.org

The Stress Reduction Clinic
Center for Mindfulness
University of Massachusetts Medical Center
55 Lake Ave. North
Worcester, MA 01655
(508) 856-2656

(United Kingdom)

International Stress Management Association
P.O. Box 348
Waltham Cross EN8 8ZL
07000 780430
www.isma.org.uk

TEEN HELP

ADOL: Adolescent Directory Online

Includes information on eating disorders,
depression, and teen pregnancy.
www.education.indiana.edu/cas/adol/adol.html

Al-Anon/Alateen
1600 Corporate Landing Parkway
Virginia Beach, VA 23454-5617
(888) 425-2666
(888) 4AL-ANON
www.al-anon.alateen.org

Focus Adolescent Services: Eating Disorders
(877) 362-8727
www.focusas.com/EatingDisorders.html

Future Point
A nonprofit organization that offers message
boards and chat rooms to empower teens in the
academic world and beyond.
www.futurepoint.org

Kids in Trouble Help Page
Child abuse, depression, suicide, and runaway
resources, with links and hotline numbers.
www.geocities.com/EnchantedForest/2910

Planned Parenthood
810 Seventh Ave.
New York, NY 10019
(212) 541-7800
(800) 230-PLAN
www.plannedparenthood.org

SafeTeens.com
Provides lessons on online safety and privacy;
also has resources for homework and fun on the
Web.
www.safeteens.com

TeenCentral.net
This site is written by and about teens. Includes
celebrity stories, real-teen tales, an anonymous
help-line, and crisis counseling.
www.teencentral.net

TeenOutReach.com
Includes all kinds of information geared at
teens, from sports to entertainment to help with
drugs and eating disorders.
www.teenoutreach.com

Hotlines for Teenagers

(United States)

Girls and Boys Town National Hotline
(800) 448-3000

**Childhelp National Child Abuse Hotline/
Voices for Children**
(800) 422-4453
(800) 4ACHILD

Just for Kids Hotline
(888) 594-5437
(888) 594-KIDS

National Child Abuse Hotline
(800) 792-5200

National Runaway Hotline
(800) 621-4000

National Youth Crisis Hotline
(800) 448-4663
(800) HIT HOME

Suicide Prevention Hotline
(800) 827-7571

(United Kingdom)

Alateen (for teens with alcohol concerns)
020 7403 0888

Anti Bullying Campaign (counseling and advice)
020 7378 1446

Careline (counseling and advice)
020 8514 1177

Family-line UK (for families in crisis)
0845 756 7800

National Association for Children of Alcoholics
0800 567123

<u>(Canada)</u>

AIDS/ Sexually Transmitted Diseases Info
(800) 772-2437

Gambling Help Line
(800) 665-9676

Kid's Help Phone
(800) 668-6868

VOLUNTEERING

City Year
20 West 22nd St., 3rd Floor
New York, NY 10010
(212) 675-8881
www.cityyear.org

STAY CONNECTED

USE YOUR VOICE

SPEAK UP

www.jessicaweiner.com

about the author

J essica Weiner is a motivational speaker, author, talk-show host, and performer who has provided programming to millions of audience members nationwide. She's the author of ten social-issue plays and a frequent contributor and guest columnist in magazines. She travels throughout the country, speaking to junior high and high schools, colleges, community groups, companies, and policy makers.

Jessica is president of Parallax Entertainment, a new media company specializing in creating television, film, and theatrical events that uphold and embrace the human spirit. She's developing a national talk show that will reach people through laughter, tears, grace, and candid dialogue.

Hmm, what else don't you know about the author?

Jessica is a Scorpio who loves strawberries and the movie *Grease*. She misses her cat, and she loves the Greek Islands. When she's not busy changing the world, she likes to walk on fire.

For more information, check out **www.jessicaweiner.com**

✱ ✱ ✱

✳ ✳ ✳

We hope you enjoyed this Hay House book.
If you would like to receive a free catalog featuring additional
Hay House books and products, or if you would like
information about the Hay Foundation, please contact:

Hay House, Inc.
P.O. Box 5100
Carlsbad, CA 92018-5100

(760) 431-7695 or **(800) 654-5126**
(760) 431-6948 (fax) or **(800) 650-5115 (fax)**
www.hayhouse.com

✳

Published and distributed in Australia by:
Hay House Australia, Ltd. • 18/36 Ralph St. • Alexandria NSW 2015
Phone: 612-9669-4299 • *Fax:* 612-9669-4144
www.hayhouse.com.au

Published and distributed in the United Kingdom by:
Hay House UK, Ltd. • Unit 202, Canalot Studios
222 Kensal Rd., London W10 5BN • *Phone:* 44-20-8962-1230
Fax: 44-20-8962-1239 • www.hayhouse.co.uk

Published and distributed in the Republic of South Africa by:
Hay House SA (Pty), Ltd., P.O. Box 990, Witkoppen 2068
Phone/Fax: 2711-7012233 • orders@psdprom.co.za

Distributed in Canada by: Raincoast
9050 Shaughnessy St., Vancouver, B.C. V6P 6E5
Phone: (604) 323-7100 • *Fax:* (604) 323-2600

✳

Sign up via the Hay House USA Website to receive the
Hay House online newsletter and stay informed about what's
going on with your favorite authors. You'll receive bimonthly
announcements about: Discounts and Offers, Special Events,
Product Highlights, Free Excerpts, Giveaways, and more!

✳ ✳ ✳